The Secret History of Everyday Stuff

Benedict le Vay

Copyright © 2015 Benedict le Vay

ISBN: 1511844485
ISBN-13: 978-1511844482

ONE PARTICULAR HOUSE ('Easier to find than Random House'),
LONDON, AMAZON and KINDLE

FOREWORD

You don't have to paddle up the headwaters of the Orinoco to be surprised by something utterly amazing. You don't have to search the markets of Samarkand and trawl the back streets of Mandalay to find the almost unbelievable, the compellingly curious, the utterly enlightening or the irresistibly odd.

You just have to look in your own store cupboard. Your food and drink; your household appliances, your medicines; your own home and street; in your country, your business, your daily transport; the very words you use every day.

That's what this book is about. Finding the utterly extraordinary in the ordinary. Dip into any of the topics and you'll soon be hooked. It's time to make the mundane marvellous...

ACKNOWLEDGMENTS

Robin Popham, Sir Michael Caine, Lawrence Webb, Bill Smith, Dr Phil Hammond, Simon LeVay. Picture research and credits: Septimus H. G. Zellwegger. Wikimedia, Imperial War Museum. Any mistakes are entirely my fault, however, and I would be most grateful for feedback/suggestions/corrections by email to benlevay@aol.com, just as readers have kindly done for my other books. Brickbats, brainwaves or bouquets, chuck them all this way!

By the way, BTW in this book means 'by the way'. It appears rather a lot, BTW.

Cover picture: JAMES BOYER SMITH
www.jamesboyersmith.com

CONTENTS

1 Household stuff: The startling secrets in your cupboards

YOUR LIGHT IS DARK: Fluorescent lightbulbs, such as energy saving bulbs, when apparently on, are off almost as much as they are on. Because they flicker with alternating current, they are completely dark 50 times a second. If you take a very fast exposure photo under such lighting, it may turn out all black. The old tungsten type bulbs with a coil of wire work by becoming white hot, so they don't cool down and go dark when the alternating current changes direction.

ENERGY-SAVING bulbs don't always save energy. In a winter home with thermostat-controlled heating, the waste heat of old-style bulbs is simply made up by burning more heating fuel if you fit the new ones. Plus you can't dim them, which would have saved energy. And in a toilet or somewhere briefly illuminated, they can use more because of starting current needed. Plus they use more to manufacture.

NOT A FOON: A combination spoon and fork used is a spork. Films set in England depicting Tudors, or earlier, eating with knife, fork and spoon are wrong. The fork arrived as late as 1608 - people before that used knives and fingers. Spoons had been around since Roman times.

QUARTZ AND PINT POTS: You wouldn't have wanted the world's first electronic quartz timepiece on your wrist. It filled a whole room. In 1927 a Bell Telephone Company engineer called Warren Marrison developed an accurate clock based on the fact that a quartz crystal vibrates at 100,000 times a second when subject to an electric current. Eventually, this type of clock, somewhat reduced, replaced

mechanical clocks at observatories and scientific laboratories. But it was not until half a century later that quartz watches became commonly available.

T-TRULY C-C-COLD: If it's very cold and your thermometer is showing minus 40 degrees, but you're not sure if it's f-f-Fahrenheit (freezing 32, boiling 212) or Celsius (0 and 100), it doesn't matter. It would be the same.

COLD FRONT: You can't manufacture cold. You can merely move heat, which is why fridges are warm at the back. Thus you can't easily air condition deep London Tube trains. It would make the system hotter. Fans don't cool rooms, they heat them slightly. It just *feels* cooler on the skin. That's why it's bonkers to leave them on while you're out.

ICE isn't slippery. Which is why ice skates need blades, to melt quickly enough a thin layer of water, which *is* slippery (as we often find out less quickly, while walking on it). Scott of the Antarctic found out how slippery ice isn't in 1912 when man-hauling sleds to reach the South Pole in temperatures so cold that the ice wouldn't melt under the runners. It was like dragging sleds over sandpaper. They all died because they thought ice was slippery.

FREEZING BOGNOR: Lec refrigerators, a British brand from the 1940s to today, was so successful that it sold fridges to Eskimos. It was sometimes thought to stand for London Electricity Company, which was a mistake. Sussex seaside fish and chip shop owners Charles and Frank Purley decided they could make chillers to keep their fish fresh – at Longford Road, Bognor Regis, hence Longford Engineering Company, hence Lec. In 1946 they set up a factory nearby and acquired a light aircraft which, bizarrely, was used to make repair calls on customers, who were asked if there were any big fields nearby where the repairman could land. Clearly it was still a luxury for the British, for by 1956 only 8 per cent of households had a fridge, whereas 80 per cent of American homes did.

THAT'S WIFE: Another aviator, RAF engineer Ken Wood, thought up the first multitask food mixer in 1947, hence the Kenwood Chef. This early advertising slogan is probably not used much nowadays: 'The Chef does everything but cook - that's what wives are for!' Er... right.

SCRAMBLED SMEG: Beko appliances are Turkish made and for some reason don't appear under the parent company's name, the Koc company. Perhaps because it's easier to ask for a 24inch long Beko. The equally odd-sounding Smeg fridge company also has a long pedigree. It was founded by Italian Vittorio Bertazzoni in 1948 as Smalterie Metallurgiche Emiliane Guastalla (metal enamelling factory in the village of Guastalla, Reggio Emilia).

GERMANESE PRODUCTS: In the 1970s British consumers thought Japanese and German products superior, not totally without reason, as British manufacturing was going through a bad patch. One of the most popular electronics brands was Matsui, accompanied by a rising sun logo. It was the own brand for Dixons and about as Japanese as Yorkshire pudding. Equally, Moben kitchens were as German as Cornish pasties, but at least sounded German. Dixons, by the way, was founded by C. Kalms and M. Mindel who wanted to put their names above the first shop in Southend in 1937. There was space for only six letters, so they grabbed a phone book and chose the first six-letter name they found. They didn't want to sound German back then!

SHARP might seem not a very apt name for a home electronics company. But it was great for a company making the first propelling pencils. Japanese engineer Tokuji Hayakawa invented the first mechanical pencil, which was marketed as 'Sharp'. He used profits to create the Hayakawa Electric Company, which still trades as Sharp.

THERE was no Mr Russell Hobbs who invented the electric kettles of that name. But there was a William Morris Russell, born 1920, (named after the Arts & Crafts doyen, not the car inventor also called William Morris) and Peter Hobbs, born 1916, who after war service together made the first automatically cutting-off kettle, the K1, in 1956.

NESCAFE Blend 37, which legend links to some dramatic Le Mans race involving the 37th lap in 1937, was in fact less romantically merely the 37th blend tried. A 99 ice cream (in Britain that is one with a chocolate Flake stuck in the soft ice cream) was equally disappointingly called after the specification for the Flake: 99mm long. After decimalisation of currency in 1971, unscrupulous traders pretended to newly arrived tourists that this was the price – about four times the correct one.

THROWING A FRISBEE should be throwing a Morrison. Walter Morrison had already thought of making saucer-shaped objects for people to throw and catch, when he saw Yale University students playing catch with thin flat pie dishes made by baker William Russel Frisbie and stamped with that name. They would shout 'Frisbie!' as they threw one. However those became dented and sharp; the shape was not as aerodynamic as his models, he thought. But he named his own product Frisbee. With his wartime experience of plastics he moulded a shape that would stay aloft longer than any ball. The first plastic was brittle and shattered; a flexible one was found. They flew out of shops.

FAMILIAR NAMES FROM HAPPENSTANCE: Mr Wait and Mr Rose formed Waitrose, Asda came from Associated Dairies. Ekco radios popular in the mid 20th century in Britain were in fact formed of the owner's fortuitous initials: Mr EK Cole. On the other hand the great aviation firm Avro, which built the war-winning Avro Lancaster bombers, resulted from a cock-up. The owner's name A.V. ROE was being painted on a hangar at Brooklands and the painter didn't leave enough room for the E. Roe had made the first all-British powered flight. Lesney, the firm behind Matchbox toys, was named by welding together the Christian names of founders Leslie and Rodney Smith.

GREAT KINGS IN YOUR DRAWERS: Each king in a pack of playing cards is said to show a great ruler from history. Spades - King David, Clubs - Alexander the Great, Hearts – Charlemagne, Diamonds – Julius Caesar.

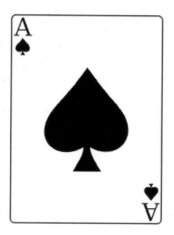

ACE OF SPADES: The harbinger of death. There was a government tax or duty on playing cards, and the penalty for forging an ace of spades was death (see Page 174). The 6 of Diamonds is known as the Curse of Scotland, because a king wrote a death warrant on the back of one.

CARDS ON THE TABLE: Playing cards have been around for longer than most people think. They were banned by the Church in 1377, so they must have been already popular by then. They were already associated with immoral activity (gambling) and like today, they had four suits. Unlike many others forms of art, playing cards are today ephemera - that is, printed material designed to be thrown away - so few complete sets of 52 survive from antiquity, and incomplete sets were usually discarded. The design is amazingly constant, because of the superstition and conservatism of card players. 'A 1450 French Queen of Spades is the same, essentially, as a 2015 Queen of Spades by Waddingtons,' said one expert.

TEFLON FRYING PANS: This material wasn't discovered in the space programme, as urban myth has it, but accidentally by Roy Plunkett in 1939 while looking for a new refrigerant. It took a housewife to suggest putting it on saucepans in 1954. It is the only surface onto which a gecko cannot cling upside down. If burnt, fumes are lethal to birds.

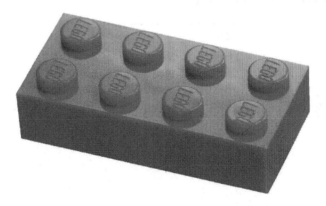

LEGGO! At more than 230 billion Lego bricks so far produced, everyone in the planet could have 37.5. In the 1930s a Danish wooden toy company named itself from the Danish words 'LEg GOdt' which means play well. Later it was realised that it means 'I read' in Latin. They made their first brick in 1953. The second one followed immediately, otherwise it would have been rather futile.

SWEET FA: Although the first tin can was invented by British merchant Peter Durand in 1810, the can opener wasn't invented and patented until 1858 (by American Ezra Warner). But the tin cans didn't stay on the shelf all those years. Made by hand and far thicker than today's models, they had to be opened with a hammer and chisel. The early cans were used by explorers and the Royal Navy in situations where fresh food was not available.

This gave rise to the expression 'Sweet FA' which was not, as is commonly believed, based on a swearword. A young girl called Fanny Adams was gruesomely murdered in Alton, Hampshire - the body was hacked about and bits left all over the place. Not long afterwards, sailors in the Royal Navy opened their first cans of meat, looked at the contents and exclaimed with the black humour of service life: 'Sweet Fanny Adams!'

At first, tin cans were made by a skilled tinsmith at six tins per day. Today one machine can make 1,500 an hour. They are still known as tin cans, although they are in fact either steel or aluminium and contain no tin. Nine million are recycled every hour worldwide.

DUCT TAPE, not duck tape, was invented during World War II (and thus originally available only in Army green) and is renowned for its flexibility, stickiness and tearability, which is down to a combination of cotton weave, plastic backing and a rubber-based adhesive. But some must be better than others – you hope – because in the USA there is a grade called Nuclear Tape, used in atomic power plants, and 200mph Tape, used in racing cars.

LEAD IN PENCILS: These are dangerous because of the poisonous lead, it is commonly believed, and schoolchildren are warned not to suck the things for fear of being struck dumb or dead. In fact they don't have and never had lead in, but contain graphite was once known as 'German lead'. Hence the confusion with the poisonous heavy metal. Chewing pencils is no more dangerous than chewing any other bit of wood. However a 'homeopathic dowser healer' was said by a newspaper to have cured Princess Diana of 'poisoning' which 'affected her posture' after an incident, which she allegedly recounted, as a schoolgirl when the point of a pencil had broken off and flown into her face, somehow poisoning her. In fact any such point would be harmless, in terms of poison. What this says about the credulity of newspapers, their readers, alternative therapists and princesses is a moot point.

MASKS ON: The deadly phosgene gas, which killed thousands in World War I attacks, can be accidentally replicated by burning certain (but not all) refrigerants in freezers and air con systems. Doctors noted this when casualties were admitted with gas attack symptoms after brazing refrigeration pipes under repair.

WHAT A SQUIRT: Inkjet printers were discovered by a careless engineer who put his hot soldering iron on a pen which then squirted a drop of ink out.

SCOTCH tape arose from an insult, meaning mean. The masking tape made by Minnesota Mining & Manufacturing (which gave us 3M) was used by Detroit car manufacturers to get a clean edge where two colours met. The car bosses demanded that the price come down, so a version of the tape with no glue down the middle was made. This enraged the car makers, one of whom said: 'Take this tape back to those Scotch bosses and tell them to put adhesive all over the tape.' They did. The tape stuck. So did the name.

AVON LADIES: American salesman D.H. McConnell was trying to sell books, encyclopaedias and the works of Shakespeare door-to-door. He started giving away perfume to keep ladies interested, and soon realised he might as well forget the books, such was their reaction. Except in one respect – he named the company out of his admiration for Shakespeare, from Stratford-upon-Avon. He still hoped some literary influence would, like his cosmetics, rub off.

WELL SPOKE: Half the spokes in your bicycle wheel aren't

doing anything useful at any one time. The lower half of the wheel's spokes, being made of flimsy wire, couldn't possibly hold your weight in compression, so it is all carried by the spokes in the top half in tension. They bottom ones might as well not be there – except that, when the wheel turns, the lower spokes move up and are doing the same job for a while.

SNOTS AND FROGS: It may be disconcerting to know your house, if traditional, is held together by thousands of snots and frogs. Frogs are the indentations on bricks that not only make them lighter and cheaper but also give the mortar something to grip by fitting into, thus holding the wall together. Snots are the bits of excess plaster that squeeze through a lath ceiling and extrude into the space between the joists above (you may have seen these in an unlined attic). Snots look messy, but without them the ceiling plaster would fall down.

FROG WARS: Frogs also hold railways together. The bit of metal where two tracks join is called a frog, and battles between rival companies at these points in the 19th century were called Frog Wars. One of these, the Battle of Havant in Hampshire, for example, involved the Brighton company chaining a scrap loco to the frog and blockading a London & South Western train from approaching via a new route. Dozens of navvies armed with pick handles and shovels squared up to each other before this battle in a frog war ended.

GROUT EXPECTATIONS: Grout, today used for the white gunge that goes between tiles, is the Anglo-Saxon word for a rough porridge, which it resembles.

BREAKING GLASS: The cracks in breaking glass travel at a speed of up to 3,000mph. Glass is, however, not a solid but technically a liquid, some experts maintain. Very old glass is thinner at the top of a window than at the bottom, as it is flowing very slowly downwards, and over many millennia, holes will appear. If no one chucks a stone through it first.

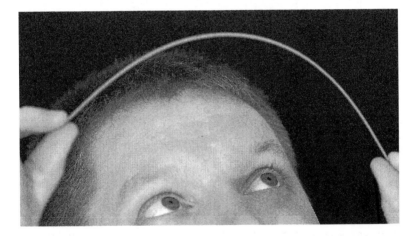

BREAKING SPAGHETTI: It is impossible to break a full-length piece of spaghetti, by bending it from both ends, into two pieces. It always makes at least three because the shock wave travels down the shaft and makes a second break. Cooked spaghetti you can bend almost as much as you like, of course.

METAL FOUNDRIES AND SMELTERS would, you might think, be wherever the ore (rock) for that metal has to be mined. Not if far more tonnage of fuel has to be used than ore in the process; for example with copper, in which case it would be near coal mines to fuel the smelters. And with aluminium, the electrically-powered smelters can never be turned off, so are usually located where there's a massive source of cheap power, such as hydro power (in Fort William, Scotland, for example).

FLOAT GLASS: When you look at lumpy medieval glass which looks as if it was poured into trays much like hot fudge, you can see completely flat modern shop window glass could never have been made like this. Nor even by rolling it out in sheets, which would have had visible distortions. Float glass was invented by Pilkington and involves glass floating on a bath of molten tin, hence it is perfectly flat.

SAFETY GLASS: Discovered by serendipity (interesting word, see Page 234) when in 1903 French scientist Edouard Benedictus dropped a glass flask containing a filmy residue of plastic. This held all the broken glass together, and modern car windscreens are made on this principle.

DISH WISH: The dishwasher was invented 100 years before it became widely used. American inventor Joel Houghton patented a wooden machine with a hand-turned wheel in 1850. The first really good model was invented in 1883 by a woman (are you surprised?), Josephine Cochran, 44-year-old wife of politician William Cochran in Illinois, after she found she couldn't trust the servants to wash her fine china without chipping it. In fact that was the original aim – to not chip the china, rather than to avoid washing them by hand. Hers could 'wash, scald, rinse and dry' in two minutes, but were aimed at large restaurants, hotels, etc. Her company eventually became KitchenAid. It was not until the late 1950s that affordable models for ordinary people started to sell.

TRUTHBRUSH: The toothbrush was invented in China in 1498. Exactly 500 years later, toothbrushes were involved in a very odd London break-in. Nothing was taken from a house broken into while a family was on holiday. It wasn't until the family played a video lying around a few weeks later they saw criminals inserting their toothbrushes in their anuses.

THE WHOLE TOOTH: Toothpaste is usually associated with whiteness. Yet the oddly named Darkie toothpaste was sold all over the Far East until the 1980s. The box and side of the tube showed a black man smiling to show a dazzling set of teeth. He was dressed as a minstrel, with a top hat. It became Darlie after U.S. sailors taking shore leave in Hong Kong and Singapore were shocked by the label.

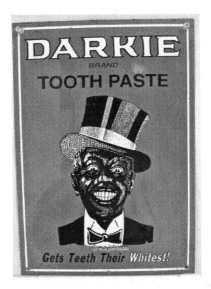

PIG BRUSH: Until 1937 toothbrushes had been made with pig bristles. And until 1892 when Dr Washington Sheffield invented the collapsible tube, toothpaste came in jars. The first TV commercial shown on British ITV in 1955 was for Gibbs SR toothpaste. It had to be screened live as there was no way of recording TV. Since it was of a brush and toothpaste tube set in a block of ice, it could only be shown so many times in a hot studio. (SR for sodium ricinoleate. It's now made by Mentadent.)

GREAT STINK: The widespread introduction of the water closet toilet, in which a U-bend of fresh water seals off the house from the pong of the sewer, might be thought to have been instrumental in cleaning up London, the greatest city in the world at the time. In fact it made things *worse*. Until this point, houses had cess pits, earth closets or soil buckets.

While not very fragrant, these allowed sewage to be taken away by the night soil men and used as fertiliser or otherwise disposed of. It was until then illegal to put this into watercourses. But as soon as the fad for water closets took hold, on the other hand, raw sewage was being run through ditches at the sides of roads, streams, canals and the Thames itself in such appalling quantities that it led to the 'Great Stink of London' in the summer of 1858. This stench, so bad that Parliament fled the capital, led to Joseph Bazalgette's great sewers that still run today, and the Thames embankments that contain them.

HAPPY CRAPPER: Many people 'know' that the verb to *crap* comes from Thomas Crapper, the 19th century British manufacturer of one of the most popular early water closets. In which case many people are wrong; it was just a happy coincidence, as the verb was used centuries before the suitably named manufacturer became a household name. BTW, water closet (meaning the water closes off the waste pipe) is about the only honest description for the white trumpet-shaped devices human beings sit on several times a day: toilet, lavatory, bog, khazi, loo, little girls' room, restroom, thunderbox, long drop, outhouse, privy are all either jokey, euphemisms or totally avoiding the truth. The French, oddly, use the initials WC although they mostly have no idea what they stand for.

IT'S A GAS: Which of these is feasible: gas iron, gas hairdryer, gas fridge, gas curling tongs, gas projectors, gas radio? Answer, all of them and they're on display at the Gas Museum in the Victorian gatehouse of an old gasworks at Aylestone Road, Leicester in the English Midlands But not the gas itself - it would be hard to pin down on a display board.

TRUE FAX: The fax machine was invented *before* the telephone. It was patented in 1843, 33 years before Bell produced his telephone, but little used. Then in the 1980s every office suddenly needed one urgently. Then in the 2000s every office suddenly didn't need one urgently.

GREAT WRONG PREDICTIONS *No 1!*
There is no reason why anyone would want a computer in their home.
Ken Olsen, President of Digital Equipment, 1977.

FIRST ELECTRIC CHRISTMAS LIGHTS: Invented by a telephone switchboard installer. The usual candles were thought to be too dangerous in such a setting so were banned. He rigged up some lights from an old switchboard around a tree, powered by a wet cell battery.

BRIGHT IDEA: We are taught Edison invented the light bulb, but in 22 documented cases light bulbs of varying success preceded him. And when Edison did finally claim to have invented the perfect bulb, for his 1878 patent, he hadn't but he needed the money. So Edison pretended he had and worked on it for more than a year until he *did* at last perfect a workable bulb. When Edison tried to market his bulbs in Britain, he found inventor Joseph Swan had got there first, so was reluctantly forced to join forces and create the Ediswan company, which eventually became Thorn lighting. (More on Edison, Page 74).

BULB FESTIVAL: The world's oldest continuously running light bulb is at hanging in the Livermore, California fire station. This 'Centennial Bulb' is located at 4550 East Avenue. The fire department claims that the bulb is at least 106 years old and has been run continuously. Because of its longevity, the bulb has been noted by The Guinness Book of World Records and can be seen working at http://www.centennialbulb.org/cam.htm - a thrilling webcam. If it hasn't gone phut in the meantime. In fact the video camera went phut after only three years, showing considerably less longevity than the bulb, but the webcam has been replaced so millions more can see a lightbulb. Illuminating stuff.

GREAT WRONG PREDICTIONS *No 2!*
The telephone wasn't much used for its first 15 years because people did not see a need for it. An MP said Britain didn't need it as 'we have enough messengers here'. Telegraph companies said in 1876 it could never replace the telegram. A Western Union report said: 'This telephone has too many shortcomings to be seriously considered as a means of communication.' Even Mark Twain refused to put any money into something he couldn't see the point of. Bad call.

THE WORD HELLO is commonly thought to have been invented with the telephone, but its much earlier use can be traced. In fact the first callers used 'Ahoy, Ahoy!' Both the inventor, aptly called Alexander Graham Bell, and the first exchange in New Haven, also aptly in Connecticut in January 1878, used 'Ahoy!'.

18

CONNECTICUT, also aptly named, could claim to have produced the world's first telephone directory, if a single sheet of fifty names on one side of a piece of paper (below) counts. The New Haven District Telephone Company's List of Subscribers came out in 1878, and didn't show any numbers; you picked up the phone and asked the operator for your connection. It did boast that shortly the telephone service would operate all night.

LIST OF SUBSCRIBERS.

New Haven District Telephone Company.

OFFICE 219 CHAPEL STREET.

February 21, 1878.

Residences.	Stores, Factories, &c.
Rev. JOHN E. TODD.	O. A. DORMAN.
J. B. CARRINGTON.	STONE & CHIDSEY.
H. B. BIGELOW.	NEW HAVEN FLOUR CO. State St.
C. W. SCRANTON.	" " " " Cong. ave.
GEORGE W. COY.	" " " " Grand St.
G. L. FERRIS.	" " " " Fair Haven.
H. P. FROST.	ENGLISH & MERSICK.
M. F. TYLER.	New Haven FOLDING CHAIR CO.
I. H. BROMLEY.	H. HOOKER & CO.
GEO. E. THOMPSON.	W. A. ENSIGN & SON.
WALTER LEWIS.	H. B. BIGELOW & CO.
	C. COWLES & CO.
Physicians.	C. S. MERSICK & CO.
Dr. E. L. R. THOMPSON.	SPENCER & MATTHEWS.
Dr. A. E. WINCHELL.	PAUL ROESSLER.
Dr. C. S. THOMSON, Fair Haven.	E. S. WHEELER & CO.
	ROLLING MILL CO.
Dentists.	APOTHECARIES HALL.
Dr. E. S. GAYLORD.	E. A. GESSNER.
Dr. R. F. BURWELL.	AMERICAN TEA CO.
Miscellaneous.	*Meat & Fish Markets.*
REGISTER PUBLISHING CO.	W. H. HITCHINGS, City Market.
POLICE OFFICE.	GEO. E. LUM, " "
POST OFFICE.	A. FOOTE & CO.
MERCANTILE CLUB.	STRONG, HART & CO.
QUINNIPIAC CLUB.	
F. V. McDONALD, Yale News.	*Hack and Boarding Stables.*
SMEDLEY BROS. & CO.	CRUTTENDEN & CARTER.
M. F. TYLER, Law Chambers.	BARKER & RANSOM.

Office open from 6 A. M. to 2 A. M.
After March 1st, this Office will be open all night.

PHONE CALL: In 1877, you could for the first time call the Oxford Fire Brigade by telephone. How reassuring. But only if you were in fire brigade engineer Neill's home. For there were only two phones in the city.

TEAR A PHONE BOOK IN HALF: The first proper telephone directory was published in London in 1880. It was a slim volume, with just 250 names and addresses – but no phone numbers. You just asked for the person by name and the operator connected you. BTW, you can still tear phone books in half and by doing so win a bet. Just tear them along the spine, vertically!

PHONE NUMBERS: Until the 1940s, prime ministers and national figures gave their numbers and their full addresses: the idea that any caller would be a nuisance hadn't occurred to them. So Winston Churchill in 1925 could be called by anyone on Paddington 1003, the Royal Family on Victoria 6913.

GOT YOUR NUMBER: The first mobile phone call was made on April 3, 1973 to the boss of a rival company to say 'Ha!' Motorola's Dr Martin Cooper called Bell's research chief Joe Engel. The housebrick-sized (and weight) handset lasted one hour and then had to be recharged for 10 hours.

DO THEY THINK WE ARE ALL IMBECILES? THE ODD LABELS ON ORDINARY THINGS:

British supermarket's peanuts: *May contain nuts.*

On an American Airlines packet of nuts: *Instructions - open packet, eat nuts.*

Marks & Spencer bread pudding: *Product will be hot after heating.*

On Tesco's Tiramisu: *Do not turn upside down* (printed on bottom).

In the manual of a chainsaw: *Do not attempt to stop the blade with your hand.*

On New Zealand swimwear: *Do not expose to sunlight, or chlorine. Do not sit on concrete surfaces. Do not allow to stay wet.*

On a 'Now You Are 2' birthday card with badge: *Not suitable for children under three.*

On logs for fireplaces in sack in U.S. service station: *Caution -- Risk of Fire.* We certainly hope so.

On a well-known brand of U.S. sleeping pills: *Warning: May cause drowsiness.* We hope so again.

On women's self-defence pepper spray: *May irritate eyes.* Yep, ditto.

On poison against mice: *Warning: Has been found to cause cancer in laboratory mice.*

That's a pity. We wanted to kill the little beggars stone dead, not merely cause hypochondriac rodents long-term health concerns.

APT AFTERLIFE: Fredric John Baur, who designed the Pringles can for crisps, had his ashes buried in one in 2008.

COAL-FIRED power stations produce about 100 times more radiation then nuclear ones, and kill way more people.

WHAT creature did the worst damage to the atmosphere since the beginning of the Earth? An enormous farting vegetarian dinosaur? A microbe that wiped out tree life? No. It was a man called Thomas Midgley Jnr., (1889-1944). He was an American chemist-engineer who not only developed the lead that could be added to petrol (gasoline) to improve engine performance, but also the first chlorofluorocarbon (CFC), for refrigeration, which he named Freon. What this means in that he condemned millions of people - including many of those reading this book, and the writer too – to being thicker, or more troublesome, than they would have been without lead poisoning from living near highways, and

also condemned thousands of Australian and New Zealanders to premature death through skin cancer caused by his CFCs damaging the ozone layer. It would, perhaps, be nevertheless uncharitable to think it apt that a man who so terribly poisoned the air we breathe should have died through suffocation, but so he did – he had invented an apparatus to help him in paralysis induced by polio, and also by lead poisoning, and became entangled with, and strangled by, the ropes. Nor is the damage he caused exaggerated. The leaded petrol was known as 'loony gas' as early as 1924, when 17 workers at plants producing the additive had already died and hundreds more been mentally damaged. Yet it wasn't until 1996 that lead in petrol was banned in the USA, and not until 2000 in the European Union. J. R. McNeill, the historian of the environment, said that Midgley 'had more impact on the atmosphere than any other single organism in Earth's history'

BRITAIN receives far more free energy – wind, tidal, hydro, solar, geothermal – than it could possibly use. If only it could be captured more efficiently!

CAMPERS in Cornwall are sometimes kept awake by 'cauliflower creak' – the noise the vegetables make at their peak growing season.

RHUBARB can be heard growing too – and is picked in vast sheds in Yorkshire's 'Rhubarb Triangle' by candlelight to keep the stems from discolouring. Which leads us on to…

2 Food: The nutty truth about things we eat

CRISPS, (IN USA, POTATO CHIPS): Created as a joke in 1853 by chef George Crum when railway tycoon Cornelius Vanderbilt was eating at his Saratoga, New York restaurant and complained that the French fries (which the British, confusingly, sometimes call chips) were too thick. Crum sarcastically sliced ultra thin bits of potato, briefly fried them and was amazed when Vanderbilt said he had a hit on his no doubt greasy hands. They were served as Saratoga Chips in restaurants as an expensive delicacy until the 1920s when an airtight waxed paper bag was invented that could be ironed shut at both ends, keeping the chips/crisps fresh. This allowed mass marketing. All that was needed after that was prawn cocktail flavouring.

MARMALADE comes, according to no less an authority than actor Sir Michael Caine, from the staff of Mary, Queen of Scots requesting her orange preserve when the Queen was ill, saying: 'Madame est malade'.

SHOCK AND THAW: Ice fishing in Canada led Clarence Birdseye to notice something odd. When he pulled a fish from the water into the way-below-zero air, it quickly froze solid. If kept frozen, the fish could be thawed weeks later and still tasted as good as a freshly caught fish (unlike slowly frozen fish which became mushy). He began experimenting with flash freezing food. He patented it in 1929. The first frozen food products appeared on the market in 1930.

FREEZE, PARTNER: Not that the idea was totally new. Francis Bacon, the philosopher and statesman, was in a coach one snowy morning in 1626 at the top of Highgate Hill in North London when he had a brainwave. He bought a hen from a poor woman in a nearby hovel, disembowelled it, then stuffed the body with snow. He had a strange new idea,

laughable to his friends, that freezing could preserve meat. Unfortunately it was soon a case of frozen Bacon as much as frozen chicken. He caught pneumonia and died. If you see a frozen chicken marked 'best before 1626', it might be the one.

AVOCADO is derived ultimately from the Aztec word *ahuacatl* meaning testicle, which it resembles. Well it does if you are male, very well endowed and dark green. Don't be surprised if any visiting Aztecs recoil at being offered testicle salad.

BASTARD BREAD: Upper crust people enjoy *bâtard* loaves of bread from upmarket British supermarkets. They might not be quite so keen if they recalled a circumflex in French usually denotes a missing S, as in hôtel, fête, bête (which should be hostel, feast, beast). So they are buying *bastard bread*. But don't worry – bastard means non-judgementally non-standard. You can buy a *bastard file,* a *bastard saw*, and newspaper columns which are not the regular width are called *bastard measure*. There's even a cannon preserved at Portsmouth's Mary Rose exhibition which with the name of the founder who *'made thysse bastard'*. It was just an irregular size, needing different balls. (A total bâtard if you were on the receiving end, no doubt). So bâtard bread is not rude, just not the standard measure. This fact will be the toast of the middle classes.

FROZEN broccoli may contain up to 59 aphids, thrips or mites per 100g on average, says the U.S. Food and Drug Administration.

PAPRIKA can be contaminated up to the following level before action is taken: 20 per cent mould count, 75 insect fragments per 25g, and for what the FDA charmingly describes as 'rodent filth', 11 rodent hairs per 25g.

AGAIN, you have to reach this level before action is taken (in other words, a little less is OK): 10 whole insects or the equivalent parts in 100g of chopped dates (that'll be the crunchy bits); 5mg of mammal droppings per pound of sesame seeds; in ground dried thyme, 925 insect fragments per 10g plus two rat hairs (is there any room left for thyme?); and delight of delights, in pizza sauce, 30 fruit fly eggs per 100g, *or* 15 fly eggs and 1 maggot *or* two maggots. Nice of them to give you a choice of flavours.

The FDA would like to point out that natural contamination (see previous item) is unavoidable in harvest by practical methods, that these are mostly not harmful but aesthetic, and that foods are not routinely contaminated at anywhere near these levels. We would like to point out that we're not hungry after all. And someone else should point out that if you want fewer chemicals, you are likely to get more natural contamination: you can't have it both ways.

YOU WILL EAT on average 23.4 tons of food in your lifetime. Including some stuff you'd rather have avoided (see above).

SWEET DEATH: An artificial sweetener could be thought of as a healthy replacement for sugar if you are fat. But not if you are a dog, to whom one such product, Xylitol, is toxic. If you leave cakes made with Xylitol around for dogs to wolf down, it can kill them.

DANISH PASTRIES are called Viennese Bread in Denmark.

HEINZ AND KODAK: Heinz tinned foods which uses the slogan *'57 varieties'* never had 57 varieties, Henry Heinz just liked the shape of a sloping *57*. The firm sells well over 1,000 varieties. BTW, Eastman similarly thought Ks attractive, so for no reason he put one at each end of Kodak, a made-up word. It worked – we remembered the name better than any other film. If you remember film at all, that is....

PEANUT BUTTER: Created by a doctor from St Louis, Missouri in 1890 for patients with bad or no teeth who couldn't manage meat, etc. In excess, helped kill Elvis Presley.

ALLSPICE is so called because it offers in one powder the tastes of cloves, cinnamon, and nutmeg. But it contains none of them and is made from the seeds of just one Jamaican pimento.

BOMBAY DUCK: One of the world's most misnamed products. An acquired taste from India, it contains no duck nor comes from Bombay, which doesn't exist officially any more anyway, as it's now Mumbai. It is a reeking dried fish. Equally Prairie Oysters, offered to gullible newcomers in some New Zealand farms, are in fact the testicles of newly castrated lambs, fried with butter.

RICE PAPER: The edible thin covering used in cakes and confectionery, is not paper and not made from rice but is made from Ginseng.

CALORIES: The explosion of a gramme of TNT has the same energy as a calorie. Which is why you have to flail your arms and legs around like a stick of demented dynamite to get rid of hundreds of them.

MARGE: Household margarine and the girl's name Margaret means the same thing – pearl-like, in origin. The artificial butter was invented in 1813 and was called Margaric acid after the Greek world for pearl. The product became known as oleomargarine, later shortened to margarine and, yes, it should pedantically be pronounced with a hard G. So *that's* why no one could butter up Margaret Thatcher.

TOMATOES: Introduced from the New World to the Old in 1556 (what *was* pizza like before that?), were once thought to be poisonous, as they are related to deadly nightshade. Along with aubergine, pumpkin and various other foods characterised as 'vegetables' on menus, they are of course fruits. In fact the tomato is the world's most eaten fruit, with more than 10,000 known varieties.

WOLF IT DOWN: The Latin name for tomato, *lycopersicon lycopersicum,* suggests this early distrust. It means 'wolf peach.' However other names have included 'the apple of love' (in France) 'the apple of paradise' (Germany) and 'golden apple' (Italy).

FRENCH INEXACTITUDE about what these various New World arrivals really were seems to continue with their menus saying Pommes Frites, literally 'Fried apples' for chips or French fries. This is an abbreviation, of course, for pommes de terre, meaning earth apples. Still wrong.

TOMATO FIGHT: On a Wednesday in late August each year Spaniards and visitors throw 120 tons of tomatoes at each other at the annual Tomatina festival in Buñol, Valencia, Spain. It's the biggest food fight in the world, (and perhaps a chance to ketchup on a few grudges). Participants are hosed down or jump in the river afterwards.

RUNNER BEANS: Grown as ornaments up garden trellises for their flowers before anyone realised you could eat them.

CARROTS: Are not carrot coloured. They were white or purple until someone introduced the orange ones as a gimmick.

BIRD BRAIN: If Elizabeth Bird had not had such a bad reaction to eating eggs, the world would not have enjoyed the reassuringly bland taste of Bird's Custard. Birmingham chemist Alfred invented the comforting pudding in 1837 so his wife could enjoy custard. But it was only after serving the treat to visitors to their home that Bird realised he might have a commercial hit.

ASPARAGUS: Roman emperors kept an express asparagus fleet for rushing the plant to them as fresh as possible. 22 per cent of people report a strange smell in their urine within half an hour of eating asparagus. Odd, in that it affects everybody but only 22 per cent of people can detect it. What's odder is that researchers must have thought it worth waving glasses of other people's asparagus wee under those noses of a wider population to find out. The word has no plural, like fish, cannon, sheep and deer. Asparagi is wrong (or are wrong).

TOMATO KETCHUP: Originally sold as a medicine. Which seemed laughable, as it was later associated with junk food - until it was recently discovered that it is naturally full of a cancer-fighting agent. A medicine after all.

PEANUTS: Other things that are not what they seem include the most commonly consumed nut, the peanut, which is not a nut but a legume and should be in the beans, peas and lentils category. Coffee is not a bean but a berry. Strawberries aren't berries because they have the seeds on the outside. Raspberries are not berries either but aggregate fruits made of drupelets.

BANANA trees are not trees but giant herbs. The fruit were initially known by the French as figs of paradise, and so perhaps bananas were the plants described in the Garden of Eden, not figs as we know them. One 14th century traveller on reaching Sri Lanka remarked that 'of the leaves of this fig did Adam and Eve make body coverings' – in which case the clothes were more extensive than we have always imagined by the modest – or rather immodest - fig-leaf of our imagination. (John de Marinolli, 1350). But then everyone 'knows' that the Bible tells of a fig-leaf. It doesn't.

BITTER TRUTH: Lemons contain more sugar than strawberries. Potatoes, raw, contain more vitamin C than oranges. So do dead rats, one scientist claims.

SQUARE BISCUIT TINS are not quite square because they used to have to be returned by the shop, which sold the biscuits on to the customers in paper bags. They would return half tins inside the big tins, so the big ones needed to be slightly longer than double that size.

PLACE NAMES are obvious in French beans, etc, but *spinach* means Spanish, *currant* means from Corinth, the *damson* is from Damascus, the *shallot* is from Ascalon in the Holy Land (also called *eschalot, scallion* etc). Equally most wines are clearly geographical, but we've forgotten that Malmsey, in which medieval kings apparently drowned their brothers, came from Malvasia in Greece.

PARSLEY: The trend for flat leaf parsley is dangerous. The curly leaf parsley was introduced because the flatleaf one can easily be confused with a poisonous common garden weed.

ARTICHOKES AND THE SUN GOD: The names of Jerusalem artichokes and heliotrope flowers (sunflowers) mean the same thing. The heliotrope plant turns towards the sun, as suggested by its Greek name - *helios* meaning sun and *trope* meaning turn. Greek myth says this arose because of an illicit love affair between the sun god Helios and a human girl. The god, having to return to Mount Olympus, turned his lover into a flower that would track him from dawn to dusk. What has this got to do with Jerusalem artichokes? Well that plant is spectacularly misnamed, being neither from Jerusalem nor an artichoke. It is a kind of North American sunflower, grown for its knobbly tuber, looking a bit like ginger, which is boiled and eaten. The Italian word

for sunflower – *girasole*, again meaning gyrate towards the sun, which the flower does – was mispronounced by English sailors as Jerusalem.

ARTICHOKES AND FARTING: The heliotrope flower has a lovely fragrance, one variety being called 'cherry pie'. The Jerusalem artichoke (above) is associated with rather different smells. Because, despite having a pleasant, nutty taste, it stores carbohydrate in a completely different form to potatoes, this artichoke can cause excessive flatulence in certain people intolerant of the compound. In 1975 a vegetarian cook in Britain advised: 'They can cause non-stop farting of real nuisance proportions, or serious discomfort in the belly. The pong can be appalling.' Nor is this knowledge anything new. A 1621 English book recorded: 'They stir and cause a filthy loathsome stinking wind within the body, thereby causing the belly to be pained and tormented, and are a meat more fit for swine than men.'

ARTICHOKES AND SEXUAL FRENZY: The other kind of artichoke, the globe one, is a kind of glorified thistle, and the name comes from the Arabic for ground thorn, *ardi shauki*. In the 16th century, women were not allowed to eat them as it was thought to do so would cause a sexual frenzy. Dr Bartolomeo Boldo wrote in the Book of Nature in 1576: '*It*

has the virtue of provoking Venus for both men and women; for women making them more desirable, and helping the men who are in these matters rather tardy.' **A vegetable Viagra, possibly.**

ARTICHOKE WARS: Globe artichokes (below) were banned from sale or display in New York briefly in the 1920s because of the 'Artichoke Wars' - the mafia was buying up all the artichokes on the market and hacking down or burning the crops of farmers in the dead of night to force the price up. By the mid-20th century, Monterey, California was calling itself Artichoke Capital of the World. The first California Artichoke Queen in 1949 was one Marilyn Monroe. Perhaps Dr Boldo (previous item) was on to something.

DOUBLE BASE: If you want to sabotage a classical music concert, feed the audience Jerusalam artichokes and coffee made, as during the last war, from roasted dandelion roots, as one St Albans hippie couple did in the 1970s. The coffee tastes pretty good, but the plant, known to Shakespeare and others as the Piss Plant or Pissabed, is a powerful diuretic. Those of the audience who aren't audibly and uncontrollably farting (see artichokes above) were wetting themselves or making for the toilet, or both at once. We do not recommend following this course of action, as you might be legally

responsible for any charges of discomfort, bowel disorders, ticket refunds, nasal assault and battery, and laundry costs.

DANDELION: The French common word for dandelion is *piss-en-lit* (wet your bed), *piscialletto* in Italian. Odd then that the English name dandelion comes from the wildly serrated leaves (below) described in the former French name, *Dents de lion*, teeth of a lion. Dandelions don't have sex; other flowers do.

STILTON: The queen of English cheese, Stilton, is celebrated in the village of that name with an annual cheese rolling ceremony, and served in the pubs there. Which is peculiar, because the creamy usually blue cheese isn't made there and never has been. In fact it's illegal to make it there, says the EU. It was created in (and is still made in) Melton Mowbray by a Mrs Frances Pawlett, who died in 1808. As that town was already better known for Melton Mowbray pork pies, it was decided to take advantage of a stagecoach stop at the Bell Inn at Stilton on the Great North Road, where some of the cheese might be sold, to give it a name. It was rindly welcomed.

GARIBALDI: A British favourite biscuit (cookie) is the Garibaldi, nicknamed 'the squashed fly biscuit' because it is very flat and contains currants. It was created for the visit of Italian liberation hero Giuseppi Garibaldi who visited London in 1864, and was so popular that many pubs were also named after him. As for the man, Garibaldi, appropriately, ousted the Bourbons. But then so did the biscuit, temporarily ousting the Bourbon as national favourite. Biscuit, BTW, means *bis cuit*, twice cooked. They aren't.

POPSICLES (ICE LOLLIES IN BRITAIN): Invented by Frank Epperson in 1905, they were originally called Epsicles,

which name, unsurprisingly, didn't catch on. He left some flavoured soda water out on the back porch overnight, with the stirring stick still in it, and in the morning he had what the Brits call an ice lolly on a stick, which his school chums loved. 18 years later, scratching around for a business idea, he remembered this and produced Epsicles in seven flavours. They were a hit, even more so when he changed the name.

PANETTONE: The Italian cakes hang upside down from racks like bats while cooling, so they keep their bosomy shape. A piece of dough is cut off in the making, called the Mother, the sign of the Cross is made over her and she is tightly wrapped and 'put to sleep' for the night before being woken up with the next day's mixing. Thus the yeast is eternal. Only one worker in each bakery is allowed to touch her, for fear of infection.

CHINESE FORTUNE COOKIES: Were not Chinese but Californian, created by local Chinese in the Gold Rush of 1849. When they were introduced into China in the 1990s they were sold as 'Genuine American Fortune Cookies'. No mention of China there.

KELLOGG'S AND SEX: Dr John Harvey Kellogg in 1884 invented corn flakes as part of a campaign to prevent masturbation. He believed the activity was a sin, and at his Battle Creek Sanatorium argued for boys' circumcision, or the wiring of foreskins closed, and in girls clitorectomy or the application of carbolic acid to that region (in fact a cruel and dangerous practice). A vegetarian, Kellogg banned flesh and spicy foods, and promoted eating plenty of fibre, drinking lots of water, and irrigating the backside with regular enemas of water and vast amounts of yoghurt. He believed spicy foods led to sin: hence his very bland cereal idea.

It is important to note the cornflakes we eat today are not John Kellogg's corn flakes, and not directly connected with his ideas. They are more interesting, with added sugar. The Kelloggs' breakfast cereals which were commercially marketed were produced by his brother Will Kellogg, (whom John Kellogg tried to sue for allegedly copying his ideas in a decades-long feud). But – ahem - they do go limp pretty quickly in milk.

ODDLY, Battle Creek was the birthplace of two more American breakfast cereal companies. Not for nothing is it nicknamed Cereal City.

TREACLE CAN BE DANGEROUS: On January 15, 1919, 21 people were killed, 150 injured and millions of dollars of damage done in the Great Molasses Flood in Boston, Massachusetts. A 50ft high storage tank burst and sent a tidal wave of 2 million gallons of the sticky stuff travelling at over 30 miles per hour through the town. Houses, offices and parts of the railway were crushed. It took more than six months to clean up the sticky moment in Boston history. Too much sweet stuff can be bad for you, it seems.

MASH QUE NADA: Scotsman Donald McLean, born 1922, had the world's largest private collection of 367 varieties of potato. Scotland's still the source of the best seed potatoes because fewer diseases flourish that far north.

WORST THING SINCE... In 1943 sliced bread was banned in the U.S., to save metal from spare parts for slicing machines that might be needed for World War II.

FISHY OUTCOME: Nearly every canteen in British factories and offices still serves fish on Fridays, although they were only ordered to do so many centuries ago by an Italian religious leader who has had no power over Britain for 500 years. It was some obscure medieval religious law designed to help fishermen. Oddly, in Britain this is still widely followed although clearly the Pope has had no writ in England after the 1530s. In fact it wasn't until 1966 that American Roman Catholics were removed from the obligation to abstain from eating meat on Fridays. British chefs, mostly not being Catholics, didn't receive that order.

SALT: What is pretty well known is that our word salary comes from salt, once as valuable as money. Hence 'worth his salt'. And that many towns such as Saltash in England used to make their own. Food snobs insist on fresh ground salt like fresh ground pepper, but this has no effect on taste, aroma, etc. They also insist on sea salt from places in populous estuaries. In which case something makes it taste a wee bit better. Food manufacturers call it 'a miracle ingredient': It's very cheap, a preservative, and makes stuff taste better than it really is.

THE REAL SHOCK of salt is a surprise to those of us who didn't do chemistry at school. It is sodium chloride and is therefore made up of sodium, an explosive metal in water, and chlorine, a poisonous element, as in gas attacks. Yet it is harmless (in the usual quantities), very stable and essential. If you add innocent oxygen to the molecule, making sodium

chlorate, you get a powerful and poisonous weedkiller, and a deadly explosive when mixed with a certain common substance. Look at the salt cellar with more respect, non-chemists!

SEL-BY DATE: A British packet of salt sold in 1995 showed a use-by before the end of that century. Some scientists believe the correct use-by date on a packet of salt produced in 2015 ought to be AD 22,015, because it is so stable. It is unlikely that any packaging would last as long as the contents.

NORANGES: An orange was originally a norange but has been mispronounced for so long that it's become an orange. Proof: Spanish for orange is still *naranja*: look on orange juice cartons in Europe and it will say *zumo de naranja*. That words beginning with an N became confused with words beginning with a vowel can be seen in the British snake once known as a nadder, now an adder. Proof: Old English *naeddre*, and in place names such as Netherfield. If the snake had been called Adder, it would have been adderfield. Ditto nuncle, napron, numpire – now uncle, apron, umpire.

ORANGE CONFUSION: The original oranges were always green. Of the eight U.S. states that have an Orange County, only one or possibly two are named after the fruit, and the rest after William of Orange, the Dutch/British monarch. New York, nicknamed Big Apple nowadays, was once called New Orange when Dutch-owned. The Dutch royal house gets its name from a town in the South of France which has nothing to do with the fruit. However, conflation of the two things gives us the orange colour in the Irish flag, representing the protestants, sometimes known as Orangemen. Only Spanish has a verb meaning to punish with oranges, or pelt with oranges: *anaranjear*.

MARMITE: If the Middle East were carpet-bombed with Marmite, or its Australian equivalent, Vegemite, peace could result. The Arabs and Israelis tend to eat unleavened bread, the argument goes, so they don't get enough vitamin B12. Deficiency of that vitamin can lead to psychosis and

aggression. Marmite is a yeast extract packed with B12. So putting Marmite on their crackers could, the theory goes, make the belligerents less crackers. Could be simplistic, but less controversial than one Far Eastern leader's serious suggestion for dealing with Afghanistan after 9/11 – carpet bombing with surplus pork fat.

WORCESTERSHIRE SAUCE: An amazingly pungent, violently aromatic concoction beloved by tomato juice drinkers and barbecuers worldwide is not only not vegetarian, having an exceedingly smelly fish in it, but was originally being rejected as far, far too ghastly to use. In fact being thrown out was the only reason it was ever a success. Neither is it of Worcestershire origins - it is pronounced Wooster, as in the city, not the county - but has its roots in Bengal, India. In the era of the British Raj, the governor of Bengal, Lord Marcus Sandys, insisted when he retired to Britain that he wanted an amazing sauce he had used in India recreated here. Its precise recipe was, and is, secret but it contains the spices tamarind, chilli, soy sauce, cloves, nutmeg, cinnamon, cardamom and that smelly little fish, the anchovy. You may or may not like it, but with those ingredients, wow, it ain't going to be boring!

LORD Sandys in 1835 visited two chemists who operated in Broad Street, Worcester, with his suggested recipe. They were John Lea and William Perrins, and they brewed up a barrel of the stuff. They were appalled at the vile results and

pronounced it 'unpalatable, red-hot firewater'. Sipping that stuff must have been a bit like being slapped in the face with a kipper while having volcanic boiling spices blown up your nose. They rolled the barrel into the corner of the cellar and got on with selling perfumes and toiletries upstairs.

A year or two went by and Lea & Perrins decided to clean out the cellar. They rediscovered the barrel of Bengal-style sauce and decided to have one more taste out of curiosity to recall how vile it was before giving the sewer rats of Worcester an olfactory rocket by pouring it away. They were amazed that it had matured into a curiously piquant yet far more mellow sauce. Like a great wine, all it had needed was time to mature. No more kippers and volcanic spices but a delicious, rich, warm and exotic taste. So in 1838 Lea & Perrins Worcestershire sauce was launched upon an unsuspecting world. The world was knocked sideways, and then rather liked it. And still does.

BRANSTON PICKLE, that stalwart of British ploughman's lunches, has darkly mysterious chunky bits that no one can quite identify. Looking at the ingredients on the label doesn't help much either. By elimination, it must be rutabaga, which sounds mysterious. This turns out to be a Canadian swede which has just the right texture for this job. Who, then was this great chef Mr Branston? It was a place, not a cook - Branston, Staffordshire, where Crosse and Blackwell started making the sticky brown stuff in 1922.

LANT: An ingredient once used in baking and beer brewing. It is stale human urine. Beer could be a single-lanted ale or double-lanted. Talk about getting pissed! Also used in drugs.

IT'S NUTS: Eat one Brazil nut a day with its brown outer skin on – not the shell – and it will stop you getting depressed through lack of selenium. Eat 100 of these nuts a day and you will stink and get fat, and therefore possibly be depressed. Eat 100 nuts without the brown covering and you will get fat with no mental effect (which may be depressing in itself). Eat a Brazil nut and the selenium pills sold by certain 'health food' shops (but not all) in recent years and you will merely excrete it, as it's not absorbable. Don't eat any selenium at all and your skin will go brown like a Brazil nut. Are they good for your health? No they can be fatal. They fall from trees in Brazil in a football-like thing which contains up to 24 of what we call Brazil nuts. This is extremely heavy, and

because it is illegal to cut down a Brazil nut tree, they can be in places where they kill pedestrians and shatter car windscreens. Nuts.

GOB STOPPER: If you had a very big mouth and an enormously sensitive detector, you could take a dental X-ray with 12lb of Brazil nuts in your gob, with the radiation going outwards through the teeth, not inwards. The nuts naturally absorb radium and have about 1,000 times more than other foods. The small quantities involved are not, however, dangerous. With about 1,300lb of Brazil nuts, if you could focus the energy somehow, you could do a brain scan.

GARLIC: Means spear-leek, obvious when you see the blade-like shoot emerge from the ground. Eat them raw and you may not have any heart attacks. Or friends.

NOT VEGGIE: Even everyday things such as beer use animal extracts - beer is often cleared with finings made from fish bladders, although these should fall to the bottom and be thrown out. And some non-meat products such as cheddar cheese are usually set using a rennet from dead cows. Then if you get into the implications of dairy production, there's the question: if the cow is giving us all her milk, what's become of the calf (especially male ones...)? Plus all those insects in herbs, spices and fruit juices (see above). It's tough being very veggie...

STEAK TARTARE, TARTARE SAUCE AND DENTAL TARTAR are all related, and all related to hell, although not too closely, and all wrongly. The Tata tribe, who were part of the Mongol horde that invaded the West in the 9th century, had the R added to link them with *tartarus* (a classical Greek pit of torment deep below the earth) and the underworld because they were considered rough and savage: hellish, in fact. The French considered the *sauce tartare* equally rough and primitive, a hellish relish. A *steak tartare* (tenderised but raw) was linked to the Tartar horsemen as they were said to keep steaks under their saddles to cushion the long rides across the steppes: on arrival they would be so tenderised

they could eat them raw, as they didn't have time to cook. A dish of the hellish barbarians (now regarded as highly sophisticated). The alchemists who discovered tartaric acid, the salts of which set hellish hard on your teeth, thought they were derived from the underworld, hence *tartar* on your teeth.

ACTING like a Tartar in English means – rightly or wrongly regarding the Asian ethnic group – being toughly inconsiderate of others' views. Which is a role actor Charles Bronson played rather well – he was, as it happens, an ethnic tatar. But then so was ballet star Rudolf Nureyev. So here are two famous Tartars – Bronson is the second!

3 Drink: The shocking stuff you pour down your throat

COCA-COLA, COCAINE AND IMPOTENCE: The recipe for Coca-Cola was invented in 1885 by Dr John Stith Pemberton in Columbus, Georgia, USA, and he called what was to become the world's No 1 soft drink by the less than snappy name, *Pemberton's French Wine Coca.* He claimed it cured impotence, dyspepsia and morphine addiction. Originally it contained cocaine from Coca and caffeine from Kola. Neither drug was frowned on at the time. Oddly, the manufacturing process uses the only coca plants allowed to be legally processed in the USA, although the process now removes the cocaine.

"LE CRITIQUE EST AISEE ET L'ART EST DIFFICILE!"

THE EAGLE
DRUG AND CHEMICAL HOUSE.
J. S. PEMBERTON,   DR. A. M. WALKER.
J. S. PEMBERTON & CO.,
WHOLESALE DRUGGISTS,
MANUFACTURING AND DISPENSING CHEMISTS,
NEXT DOOR TO J. ENNIS & CO'S HARDWARE STORE.

COCA-COLA is regarded as the all-American drink, but its founder Dr John Stith Pemberton in fact fought heroically *against* the Union and for the Confederacy in the American Civil War. After he brewed the first gallon of syrup, he carried it down the street in a jug to Jacob's Pharmacy

where it was sold with soda water. It would have stayed alcoholic if Atlanta hadn't introduced Prohibition in 1886, so Pemberton's French Wine Coca became Coca-Cola, a soft drink.

BUBBLE TROUBLE: Not that Coca-Cola's success did John Stith Pemberton much good. He sold the company in 1887 to Asa Candler (1851-1929) a wholesale druggist, for $2,300, and then died. Candler sold the company in 1919 for $25 million. Today it's worth billions.

BOTTLING IT UP: All this success had gone on without one Coca-Cola bottle being sold. Until Joseph A. Biedenham of Vicksburg, Mississippi, had a brainwave of bottling it in 1894, it was only mixed to order at soda fountains. It wasn't until the 1920s that more was sold in bottles than from soda fountains in drugstores.

THE COKE BOTTLE: The Marilyn Monroe shape of Coca-Cola bottles is based on the wrong plant. Neither the coca nor the kola plants, but on cocoa pods. The reason was that the designer couldn't find a picture of the right plants in the library, so he copied cocoa, but it was accepted by company chiefs who realised that people would recognise the shape even in the dark, (as with Ms Monroe, come to think of it).

LOVEABLE fizzy Fanta could almost be described as originally Nazi waste products. It was created by the Nazi-

era Coca-Cola company in Germany in 1940 because they couldn't get Coca-Cola syrup through the Allied blockade, (the USA wasn't yet in the war, but the Battle of the Atlantic was raging). The chiefs of the German Coca-Cola company in Essen decided to keep their plant going by inventing a new fruit flavoured drink, and they employed two waste or rather by-products - apple fibre from cider pressing and whey from cheese making. The chief of the company, Max Keith, asked employees to come up with a name using Fantasie, meaning imagination, and salesman Joe Knipp adapted this to make Fanta. The drink was successful throughout the war and the trade mark was later bought by the parent company in the USA; modern ingredients are different, with more than 100 flavours sold in more than 100 countries.

NAZI COLA? Although Coca-Cola had been popular with the Nazis, and Germany was the company's most successful foreign operation up until the war, it would be wrong to depict its German operation as in any way pro-Nazi. In fact one of the impetuses for inventing Fanta was that a German rival, Afri-Cola, was trying to depict Coca-Cola as Jewish connected (by producing kosher labels or bottle tops from U.S. marketing), and therefore to be shunned by the crazed Nazi ideology of the day.

Max Keith, a German who took over for the duration after the American boss died, firmly resisted pressure to join the Nazi Party and kept the Fanta profits for the American parent company at the end of the war. Oddly, having been accused of being Jewish-linked by Nazi competitors, Coca-Cola was accused of being anti-semitic after the war because of a perceived reluctance for several decades to open a bottling plant in Israel, which critics claimed was to avoid a boycott in Arab countries.

DYSPEPTIC PEPSI: It is more than 100 years since chemist Caleb Bradham decided on a new name for the product he had called Brad's Drink. But why did he choose Pepsi-Cola? Cannily, he realised that only the first half of Coca-Cola, rivals 12 years before, was a trademark. While products such as Koca-Nola, went down the plughole in the courts for imitating the older drink's name, Pepsi-Cola survived. The first half of the name indicated it was supposed to remedy dyspepsia.

PROMOTION BOMBS: Dyspeptic might be what a group of enterprising individuals felt in 1996 when they bought truckloads of Pepsi to get 7 million points in a promotion. According to a possibly jokey TV commercial, this number of points were needed to buy a fully-equipped brand new fighter jet. The investors realised that the warplane cost $33 million but the points only $700,000. They could flog the jet to some mad tyrant at half price and get $16,000,000 in loose change. The ensuing court case shot down the whole thing in flames.

DANDELION AND BURDOCK: This British soft drink contains neither plant. The Scottish soft drink Irn-Bru, pronounced 'iron brew' and a startling orange colour, is the most popular imported drink in Moscow. Idris brand soft drinks were named after the Welsh Mountain Cader Idris, but have nothing to do with it. Another popular soft drink is Kia-Ora. It is a Maori greeting from New Zealand meaning 'Be healthy'. It has never had anything to do with Maori or New Zealand. The company's first product was chilli cordial.

FERMENTING Champagne a second time, in the bottle, is what gives its pressure and fizz, but it produces a mucky sediment. This is removed without losing the pressure by inverting the bottle for a long time, freezing the neck, removing the temporary crown cap, digging out the ice with the sediment in, inserting the proper cork, bending over the cork top and wiring it on.

BRANDY is often regarded as a posh, but was originally a way of treating third-rate wine that wasn't worth transporting, by heating and collecting the distillation. Hence Dutch called it *brandewijn* 'burnt wine', which Brits mispronounced 'brandy'.

FIRST TRADEMARK: It was a rotten New Year's Eve for one Bass brewery employee on December 31, 1875. He waited up all night to be first in the queue the next morning to register the world's No 1 trademark. It was the red triangle on Bass beer bottles. This had the advantage of being simple to stamp on bottle labels, crates, etc., to be understood by the illiterate and the foreigner, and above all it was brilliantly visible at a distance.

THUS bottles of Bass can clearly be seen alongside champagne in Edouard Manet's lovely painting of 1882, *Bar at the Folies-Bergere* (detail, below). Then Picasso had the Bass label in no fewer than 40 paintings. The Spanish artist Juan Gris put the Bass label in his paintings, even calling one of them *La Bouteille de Bass* (1925). Six other artists included the trademark in paintings and woodcuts. Levi Wells Prentice produced a painting *Still Life With Basses Ale* (1890). You can't buy publicity like that any more.

SECOND TRADEMARK And trademark No 2? Bass got that too – the Bass Red Diamond for a strong ale. Totally forgotten.

TIPSY: Heineken beers simply but subtly tilted back the three Es in its label to make them appear more smiley and less formal. It now has something to smile about - it owns 130 breweries in 65 countries. Helping us all get tilted.

THE GUINNESS brewery lease in Dublin runs until the year 10759 because it was let for 9,000 years at £45 a year in 1759. Bargain.

CARLSBERG Special Brew is a lager beer so strong that it is ideal for those who want to get canned, as it were. But its origins are grander: it was created specifically for Sir Winston Churchill, as Denmark's thank you for Britain's fight for freedom in World War II. Soon forgotten by its drinkers, like everything else ...

BRUT on Champagne labels, meaning very dry, may amuse English speakers who think it sounds like brute, as in brutal. But it *does* mean that, and it's the fault of the English. Until the mid-19th century, Champagne was always sweet or very sweet, as were all pre-dinner drinks, such as sherry or Madeira. They added syrup if the vintage wasn't sweet enough. Then an enterprising vintner realised the English would like something drier. Most champagne houses declared they would never allow anything as brutally dry – *brut*, unrefined, which is what they thought of the English – to pollute their cellars, but the change spread and now they all make *brut*. Sweet sparkling wines are now thought of as relatively plebian, even by the French.

EXPLOSIVE FIZZ: In the early days of Champagne making, it was hard to get the volatility right for the strength of the bottles. Workers in the cellars would wear iron masks or chain mail because from 20-90% of a particular vintage

would explode. As bottles had to be rotated an eighth of a turn each day, it was dangerous work.

TEA BAGS were invented by people making a mistake. Salesman Thomas Sullivan of New York City used them to send samples to his customers in 1904 instead of sending tea in more expensive tins. Unexpectedly, they put the whole thing in the pot or cup, then liked the convenience of not having to clean out the pot or strain out all the leaves, told Sullivan how brilliant 'his' idea was, and the tea bag was born.

STARBUCKS COFFEE: Is named after a character in the novel *Moby Dick*. In fact one of the three founders of Starbucks wanted to name it after the ship in the book, *Pequod*, but the other partners objected. Looking around their home city, Seattle in Washington state, they noticed a promising-sounding place called Starbo, and so settled on the character from the book, the first mate, Starbuck. Their adoption of the Siren, the mermaid figure on their logo, may not have been quite so wise. Didn't she in legend use her charms to lure sailors to their deaths on the rocks? Devious sociopath wants to murder you? Or maybe the thinking is: 'Got wrecked last night? Come in and have a coffee.'

WINE BOTTLES: The standard 750ml wine bottle is set at that sometimes inconvenient measure because that is all a skilled glass-blower could make in one single puff. It is a quantity which makes two people illegal drivers in some countries, yet for one person often leaves an annoying amount which will soon waste if you don't finish it. Wine growers like wine boxes (known as 'riot packs' by young New Zealanders) which appear to the consumer to avoid this wastage. They don't, totally, because atmospheric pressure means that a wine gobletful of wine always remains in the bladder inside when the tap stops running. If you want to test this out, stab the box and bag right through, when apparently empty and get your 'free' glass out of the tap. Just don't cut yourself if you've had a few...

CANNED fruit juice is allowed to contain up to 9 per cent mould count and 19 fly eggs or three maggots per litre, says the U.S. Food & Drug Administration.

TEA made the Industrial Revolution possible in Britain. People had to move to towns where water from pumps in the street would be contaminated by sewage, bringing cholera and other fatal illnesses then not understood. Therefore the populace, even children, had to drink beer all the time, or die. Other forms of alcohol such as gin were very cheap and very strong. The increasing adoption of tea, however, meant workers were alert enough to operate machinery and the boiled water made it safe. Heavy taxes on tea, which had caused smuggling (and the American revolution), ended in 1784, just in time for industrialisation to get going.

SCANDAL BROTH, PRATTLE BROTH AND CHATTER BROTH: All three in an 1811 London dictionary of slang are defined as one familiar thing - tea.

ROUND TOTAL: The reason milk cartons are square whereas soft drinks are sold in round bottles might seem to be that the latter are pressurised when carbonated. But increasingly soft drinks such as squashes and mineral waters aren't carbonated. True, milk isn't often drunk direct from the carton – except by sneaky teenagers – so it doesn't need to be so holdable. But here's the real reason: shelf space for milk is expensive, being refrigerated, and a square carton wastes less of it. Which is why when soft drinks and juices start needing refrigeration - as with smoothies - they often switch to square cartons, and thus from glass, tins or plastic, which can be round, to paper, which can't.

CAMP COFFEE: A treacly bottled concentrate of coffee, chicory and sugar, originally designed to help soldiers in the field get a hot drink (slogan 'Ready, Aye, Ready'), had its label quietly redesigned in 2006. It used to show a kilted Scottish soldier sitting outside his tent being served this drink by a turbanned Indian. The new label (below right) shows them sitting down in a more equal relationship. Perhaps the two soldiers will be snogging one day, a wag on social media suggested!

CAMP INDEED? There may have been schoolboy jokes about the other meaning of 'camp' in Camp Coffee (see previous item) – well they seemed to be in skirts! But for the Scottish military hero of the day whom the label is thought to depict, it all became seriously unfunny. Major General Sir Hector Archibald MacDonald, born 1853, was a great war hero indeed, with monuments to him all over Scotland, but the end of his career was marred by accusations of sex with local boys in what is now Sri Lanka. When these made the papers, he shot himself in 1903.

CORONA: A popular British soft drinks brand from the 1920s to the 1990s, Corona had as its logo a crown, which you could see if you looked closely showed seven of the old wire-topped carbonated bottles. A Corona product still being marketed is Tango. Both words are Latin, meaning 'Crown' and 'I Touch'. Odd that: the latter takes two!

POP FACTORY: The original name for the Corona company (last item) was Welsh Hills. Their factory at Porth, Rhondda Valley, South Wales, (above) which became redundant when the company was taken over, was brilliantly rebranded as a music recording and arts centre called 'The Pop Factory' - pop being British slang for both the music and the soft drinks.

DOES the energy drink Red Bull contain any bull? Yes - or at any rate a compound first extracted from one. Taurine, which is on the list of ingredients, was first extracted from the bile of a bull, as the name suggests. Whether the bull was red is not recorded.

BOMBAY Sapphire gin is made in exotic Basingstoke.

DOM PERIGNON is widely credited by the French for inventing champagne, and the method which fixed the bubbles in the wine. Locals proudly show you the monk's statue (below) at Epernay, Champagne-Ardenne. In fact the master blender of wine was trying to *get rid of* the bubbles, because they wasted wine by bursting the bottles. It was an Englishman, Christopher Merret, who found out how to control the double fermentation and keep the sparkling wine in extra-strong bottles made in Newcastle.

4 Clothes: Can you unravel these odd garments?

WARP AND WEFT OF HISTORY: Tourists driving through Brittany may note the oddly named town of Guingamp on their way to a picnic probably without realising that it gave us the cloth they might spread out for their meal, *Gingham*. Some of the places in England that gave us common textile names are more obvious - *Axminster, Worsted* or *Wilton*, the latter village once so important it gave us the county name, Wiltshire - but others around the world not so. The cloth of Nîmes was serge de Nîmes - *denim*. Hesse gave us the coarse sacking, *hessian*; Damascus, *damask*; Cambrai, *cambric*; Fustat (Egypt), *fustian*; Bocking, *bockings*; Ypres, *diapers* and Calcutta, *calico*. Things named after places are toponyms.

CORDUROY, however, means cloth of the king, *cord du roi*.

CRIMEAN WAR: Must have been cold - it and its British participants gave us three woollen garments, Raglan, Balaclava and Cardigan.

TWO NATIONS divided by a common language, as the old joke goes about the U.S. and Britain, certainly applies to clothes. Cue much embarrassment. Brits would be mortified if anyone saw their pants (underwear) while Yanks would find it funny that a man would want to put on a jumper (Americans mean pinafore dress, Brits mean sweater). Equally a glimpse of suspenders could be thrilling to a heterosexual Brit male (they hold up stockings on the upper thigh of a woman and are normally well hidden) while not so to average Americans (they hold up male pants, which in British are braces holding up trousers).

CRIMPLENE might sound like a synthethic material named to suggest it resists crumples. In fact the ICI factory which produced it was located in the Crimple Valley.

RUBBER SHOE: The soles can be recycled to make basketball courts and all-weather soccer fields, while such shoes in turn can be made out of car tyres.

TRILBY HAT: Comes from the 1894 gothic horror novel *Trilby*, by English writer George du Maurier, via a West End play of the story, where a character wore a hat of this style. The town of Trilby, Florida was named after the heroine of the novel, not the hat. People who have worn trilbies include Inspector Clouseau, James Bond, The Blues Brothers, Frank Sinatra (above), Kojak, Pete Doherty and Justin Timberlake. Plus women such as Madonna and Zara Phillips.

BTW, the novel also gives us the name of Svengali for an older man who guides and controls a younger woman, as the character Svengali does to Trilby in the book. The book *Trilby* also coined the phrase 'in the altogether', meaning naked. The author came up, too, with 'bedside manner' for how a doctor behaves, while writing for *Punch* magazine. BTW, he was grandfather not only to the novelist Daphne du Maurier who wrote *Rebecca*, but also to the five orphaned boys who became the Lost Boys in the book, play and film *Peter Pan*.

THE real reason Trilby hats (previous item) suddenly became popular in about 1955 was that the roofs of American cars

were lowered to make them more stylish and streamlined. This made the Fedora – the wider brimmed and taller crowned hat such as that worn by Indiana Jones in the movies – totally impracticable.

PANAMA HATS: Are not and never have been made in or even mainly sold from Panama. They are made in Ecuador, or the best ones are. In 1925 they were made compulsory in Turkey in a bid to ban the traditional fez. Churchill, Khrushchev and Humphrey Bogart wore them.

HAT WEARING: Up to 1950 was almost universal and often denoted social class, eg in Britain, top hat - toff, bowler hat – foreman, cloth cap – manual worker. Look at a picture of an early 20th century horse race and *everyone* of either sex wore a hat. The biggest push towards the hatless society was the sight of President Kennedy at his inauguration bare-headed. People realised they didn't really have to wear hats.

BLAZERS: The flame red jackets worn by the Lady Margaret Boat Club at St John's College, Cambridge, gave rise to the word 'blazers'.

SHOE SIZE: Where do those strange numbers originate? In Britain, shoe size is measured in barleycorns – a medieval measurement which defines an inch as three barleycorns.

AMERICANS ARE BASTARDS! British and American tie stripes slope different ways because in British heraldry a stripe from top right to bottom left symbolised a bastard line in the family. To the amused suggestion that this means most American males are announcing 'I'm a bastard' one has to add that the rule didn't apply in the USA. However, some Americans know about it: the first President George Bush was careful always to wear British sloped stripes.

CRAVAT: Meant Croat, as in Croatia, where neckties came from. If they are silk, they are not vegetarian, in as much as you have to kill caterpillars to make silk.

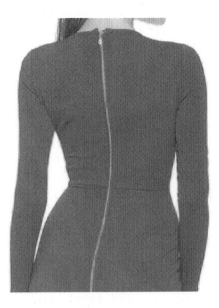

THE ZIP: or zipper was known as a 'separable fastener' or 'clasp locker' by the original patentee, American inventor Whitcomb Judson, who produced his device (not entirely original even then) in 1893, in time for the Chicago World's Fair. The biggest drawback - an apt phrase - was that it didn't work very well, it rusted shut if washed, and no one had thought of using them for clothes. The first 20 sold were for mailbags. A better 'hookless fastener' version that actually worked was produced in 1913, although they could still rust shut. Still no one had thought of using them for ordinary clothes - these were for army equipment. It wasn't until 1923, when B.F. Goodrich started using them for rubber galoshes and coined the word zipper because of the zip sound they made, that they came into any widespread use. When first used on clothes, people were given printed instructions on how to use zips.

ALDOUS HUXLEY: Features zippers prominently in his novel *Brave New World* because they hadn't yet become widely used but he thought they would. The trouble with such future-shock books, or utopias, dystopias or science fiction, is that if the prediction comes true it is boring and

ordinary to future readers, and laughable if not. The novel also predicted that people would go to completely fake lands or parks created by holiday corporations, even in different continents while ignoring the real people who live there and their culture; that they would increasingly let the state take over child rearing and interfering scientists would create designer babies; that women would become increasingly pneumatic, perhaps artificially; and everyone would go everywhere by the then equally novel helicopter, causing traffic jams in the sky while roads were empty below. Oh well, one wrong isn't too bad, Aldous, old chap. BTW, dying on the same day as President Kennedy - November 22, 1963 - was a bad move, career-wise, because no one noticed. A bit like Mother Teresa and Princess Diana dying almost together in 1997. The nun went unsung. As someone said: 'Elton John might as well have written a song called Sandal In The Bin.'

BIKINI: It is a commonly held myth that Bikini island group in the Pacific is made up of two parts. It's made up of a whole string of islands but was the base for a series of atomic bomb tests. The French inventor of the skimpy two-piece bit of swimwear at around the same time thought the bikini might have an effect a bit like an H-bomb going off.

MONOKINI was a back formation name for the outfit which is just the knickers part of the bikini, that is topless. It is grammatically wrong because it assumes the Bi- in Bikini stands for bi- meaning twice, as in binocular, monocular. It doesn't. Mankini is something even worse...

DAGGER AND MAIDS: Men's clothing has the button on the right so a right hand can withdraw a hidden dagger. Men's cloaks would have had the left flap over the right for this reason. Later it became usual because a man would button his own clothes, needing his right hand to be on the button side, whereas a lady would be dressed by a maid, so the buttons needed to be the other way round for her fingers to work them.

BRAS: Equally it would have been unseemly for a maid to fasten a woman's bra at the front, so they were stuck with back fastenings - much to the consternation of millions of men who have tried to unclip them nonchalantly while pretending to concentrate on kissing the female. Oddly 'front loaders' were tried in the 1970s but were derided by at least one woman columnist for being too forward, suggesting too easy access. Except for maternity bras.

NATURE'S IDEA: Around 1950 a Swiss mountaineer George de Mestral was walking through the woods and noticed how strongly the burs clung to his clothes, even more so to his dog's fur. Pulling them off, he realised that this principle could make a touch-and-close fastener that could compete with zips (zippers) and unlike them would not have to be aligned carefully and could put up with a large amount of dirt, damage and deformation. A French weaver obliged him by producing a cotton version that they called 'locking tape'. It was difficult to make, and not strong enough. By serendipity, de Mestral also discovered that nylon, when sewn under infrared light, formed indestructible hooks, which always returned to their shape. He called it velvet hook, *velours crochet*, or Velcro for short. Its advantage is it strongly resists sideways forces, but is easily opened by pulling outwards, and doesn't have to be precisely lined up. Great for tent flaps, quick-change theatricals, etc.

SOFT LEATHER became possible because of dog excrement. This material, known as 'pure', and urine were used in tanning up until the early 20th century, and cordwainers would pay people to collect stale and whitened dog poo. Tanneries were unpopular neighbours because of the vile smells; today more pleasant agents are used.

REAL HEELS: Women prisoners in British jails get escorted to shoe shops to choose footwear. Men are issued with black ones.

PLIMSOLL shoes are name after the Plimsoll loading line on ships, because the rubber line goes right round them.

DURING a recent affray in Dublin, looters stole all the shoes from racks outside shoe shops. They were all left footers, so useless unless there are a lot of Irish amputees (well, even then it has to be the right leg, so only half of them). By coincidence, left-footer is slang for a Roman Catholic.

A STRANGE SOLE: A Londoner called Jeremy (he won't give his last name for fear of someone stealing his collection) has 1,587 pairs of trainers (unused, in boxes). Girlfriends have threatened to leave him over his collecting habit, but he told a TV reporter 'Shoes don't answer back.' He has a Nike emblem tattooed on his ankle. 'I'm branded for life.'

ASICS sports shoes and trainers sound like a name based on 'basics'. In fact it's an acronym for A Healthy Mind In A Healthy Body, but in Latin – Animus Sano in Corpore Sano.

5 Sweets/candy: Odd facts to chew on

MALTESERS: Are the most popular confectionery item with Maltese people, although this is merely a coincidence - the name of the product derived from malt, the food, not Malta, the island. They were invented in 1936, briefly called Energy Balls and marketed also as a 'portable malted drink in a box'. Five billion a year are eaten.

MARS: Despite other chocolates or candy bars being called astronomical names such as Galaxy and Milky Way, the fact that Mars Bars are named after the firm's founder, Frederick Clarence Mars, is widely known by chocolate nuts. But the name of his horse? Snickers. A chap called A. Rocket was stopped for speeding to Mars in Slough, Berks, in the 1990s, causing much merriment at Thames Valley police HQ.

M&Ms: Inspired by Spanish Civil War soldiers who carried a hard candy-coated chocolate to avoid it melting in the heat. Some of these soldiers were encountered in Spain by Forrest Mars, son of FC Mars (above). Oddly, he was travelling with a member of the British confectionery family Rowntree. Both were impressed with the idea, but it was Rowntree who rushed home and created Smarties. Eventually Mars and Bruce Murrie bought the rights to sell this in the USA, but, as there was a different product in the States using the name Smarties, used their own surnames' initials to immortalise their partnership. The Ms are offset printed with vegetable dyes. Peanut M&Ms were not introduced until 1954, but they might have killed Forrest Mars – he was allergic to peanuts all his life, but still sold billions of them.

MILKY WAY: You can buy Milky Ways on both sides of the Atlantic, both produced by Mars, both totally different. The U.S. one is what Brits call a Mars bar while the Brits have a completely different Milky Way, a much lighter thing.

FORERUNNERS of the Milky War chocolate bar (the American version, that is) in Minneapolis candy stores of the 1930s included the less than appetising sounding Rough Rider, Chicken Spanish, Cherry Humps, Chick-O-Stick, Prom Queen, Fat Emma, Cold Turkey, and Long Boy Kraut.

KITKATS: Britain's best selling chocolate bar, KitKat, was produced by Mars's rivals Rowntree in 1935 and initially called Chocolate Crisp. The name KitKat, taken from a political club of the 18th century, was adopted a few years later. That club was started by Christopher (Kit) Catling (Cat). The KitKat bar took off and has never looked back, with mint, plain, orange, chunky etc varieties, though these have never surpassed the success of the four-finger original. Oddly, a Mars firm did produce a product called KiteKat, but it was a catfood.

ICE CREAM SUNDAE: Invented on a Sunday, hence the name, because flavoured soda drinks were not served on the Sabbath to respectable people. Lacking anything enticing to offer, Edward Berner of Two Rivers, Wisconsin, invented the Ice Cream Sundae, when he served a customer ice cream topped with the chocolate syrup that was used for ice cream soda drinks, one day in 1881. It was a Sunday, although Ithaca, New York, also claims the credit, in which case it was cherry syrup with a cherry on top. Perhaps they both had the idea.

BASSETT'S LIQUORICE ALLSORTS: Resulted from a cack-handed salesman. In 1899 their sales rep Charlie Thompson dropped a tray of samples he was showing a client, mixing up the various sweets. He scrambled to re-arrange them, and the shopkeeper thought the mixture better. Bassett's began to mass-produce the 'allsorts', and they had a hit on their hands that is still selling more than a century later, and has been imitated around the world, particularly in South Africa.

SWEET MEATS: You might assume that popular British sweets such as Liquorice Allsorts (above) and Smarties are vegetarian but in 2004 we were reminded that they were not (although, note, this has since been changed). The bright red Smarties - chocolate beans - were coloured with cochineal, which is made with an extract from a female Central American beetle, dried and crushed. Whether it was worse to see your children with merely chocolate smears on their faces or with crushed dead beetle extract dribbling down their chins is up to you. But for the squeamish or fervently vegetarian there's worse to come. Many sweets still include gelatine, which is made from animal bones.

PEPPERMINT LIFESAVERS: An American mint ring favourite, a bit like British Polo mints, owed its creation to both icebergs *and* hot weather. In 1912, at around the time life preservers (in Britain lifebelts, the ring shaped things thrown to people who can't swim) were coming into the news more and more, partly because *Titanic* had her meeting with an iceberg, American chocolate maker Clarence Crane was losing sales every summer because his products became sticky. At a chemist's store, he saw how pills were stamped out and thought of the idea of making a ring-shaped mint that would stay hard even in hot weather.

CHOCOLATE MAKERS have often turned out to be philanthropists, such as the Rowntree Trust charities in England. They also created 'model villages' - towns for their workers which were supposed to be ideal: Hershey, Pennsylvania (streets include Cocoa Avenue and Chocolate Avenue), Bournville near Birmingham, England, and Rowntree's New Earswick, York. And the triangular city of Toblerone-sur-Dimanche, Switzerland … sorry, we've just made that last one up. But that product's triangular peaks are supposed to represent the Swiss Alps, each marked with one letter of the brand if you look. And they also make the packet a lot bigger than the volume of chocolate. BTW, have you noticed the hidden bear in the mountain logo of that brand? Not convinced? It's made in Bern, 'city of the bears'. Highlighted here:

WRIGLEY, the chewing gum firm, originally made baking powder and started giving away free sticks of chewing gum with it. The customers preferred the gimmick to the original product, and so a multi-million dollar global business was born leading, among other things, to the magnificent gum-coloured Wrigley building in Chicago ... and a few sticky lumps on the sidewalks below.

HARIBO, the German chewy sweet brand, was founded in 1920 by Hans Riegel in Bonn and the name is an abbreviation of **Hans Riegel, Bonn.**

WALL'S ICE CREAM: Created solely because certain months didn't have an R in them. It was widely thought by the public before refrigeration that it was unsafe to eat any pork products in a month that didn't have an R in the name – ie the four months of the English summer. This habit stuck long after refrigeration arrived for the wealthy classes. This was a problem for the Wall's sausage company and in 1924 they sent their sausage salesmen out on tricycles (pictured above) in the summer with bins full of Wall's ice cream, using the now famous slogan 'Stop

Me and Buy One.' (Later when contraceptive dispensing machines were introduced in British pubs, wags invariably scrawled 'Buy Me and Stop One' on them). And no, the ice cream isn't made out of the pork fat. Wall's sausages and Wall's ice cream are still leading brands. Just not on the same plate, please...

MANY commercially-produced ice creams contain seaweed.

SOFT ice cream was invented by a young Oxford University chemist called Margaret Roberts. By increasing the amount of air in the product it could not only be served from a spigot to order but was also easier to eat - and more profitable. Mrs Thatcher, as she became known as Prime Minister, was later famous for licking the trade unions, coal miners, Argentine dictators, the Soviet Union and various others.

ANTRIFREEZE, which stops your car icing up, is also used on the icing of some cakes, to make it more fluffy. Polypropylene glycol can be used to improve the stability of cakes' colourful topping. More of this chemical – poisonous in certain quantities – is allowed in the USA, where it appears in a few brands of margarine, whiskey and salad dressings.

MOST liquorice is consumed in tobacco, not confectionery.

6 Inventions: Strange or silly origins of things you use daily

MAGIC NUMBERS: In 1953, a fledgling company called Rocket Chemical Company and its staff of three set out to create a line of rust-prevention solvents and degreasers for use in the aerospace industry, in a small lab in San Diego, California. It took them 40 attempts to get the water displacing formula worked out. But it must have been really good, because the original secret formula for WD-40 — which stands for Water Displacement perfected on the 40th try — is still in use today. Equally the rather different liquid Chanel No 5 was the fifth mix that Ernest Beaux submitted to Coco Chanel in 1921. Sometimes the number is a date: The AK-47 rifle was the Automatic Kalashnikov of 1947, the B-52 bomber launched in 1952. Both are still going, for good or ill. BTW, WD-40 is also a handy treatment for wasp stings and, according to a letter in *The Times*, London, good for easing arthritic knees. BTW, Mikhail Kalashnikov became obsessed with building his rifle in hospital after being shot by a superior (to the then Russian weapons) German rifle in 1942. Did he give it his best shot? Well, 75 million have been made so far in various countries, and the AK-47 has featured on four countries' flags or coats-of-arms.

THANK GOD IT'S FARADAY: We owe all these things to a punch-up in a lecture hall: radio, electric motors, dynamos, generators, refrigeration, electro-plating and many theories about space, the bending of light by magnetism, and chemical bonding being electrical. Modern life would be impossible if Michael Faraday (1791-1867) had not discovered or developed these things, but as a young man he had applied and failed to become the assistant to scientist Sir Humphry Davy, the inventor of the Davy safety lamp for miners. Davy regretted he had no job to offer the promising

67

young man, but soon afterwards Davy's assistant was sacked for fighting in the lecture hall. Faraday applied for and won the position. So important was Faraday's contribution to science that Albert Einstein kept a picture of him on his desk.

ACUPUNCTURE REPAIR OUTFIT? We owe the pneumatic tyre to a Belfast boy's testicles. Veterinary surgeon John Boyd Dunlop feared his son would be made sterile by bouncing along the roads on solid bicycle tyres, so experimented with rubber tubes and tyres, perfecting the design in 1886.

WORRIED HORSES: W.H. Fancher and C.M. French, perhaps appropriately from Waterloo, New York, in 1862 patented a combined plough (or plow) and gun. In fact it seems to have been a small cannon, and you lined it up with the plough handles, the plough share in the ground preventing the recoil as the 3lb shell went hurtling straight ... up your horse's backside (well, you were supposed to remove the horse, but what if it went off accidentally?). But why? Apparently they thought it would do for places 'subject to sudden feuds'. Feuds? In America?

QUESTION: What do film and music stars Marlon Brando (above), Danny Kaye, Michael Jackson, Zeppo Marx, Jamie Lee

Curtis and Hedy Lamarr all have in common? They have patents for their inventions. For example…

FILM STAR INVENTOR: Marx Brother Zeppo was a great inventor. As well as the vapour pad, he invented the Marman clamp which was designed to hold down cargo during transport. They are still used as quick connectors for wide-diameter fuel pipes, on space flights, and supported the atomic bomb on *Enola Gay*. He also invented medical devices - a pulse rate monitor and an external pacemaker.

MORE FILM STAR INVENTORS: Screen legend Marlon Brando patented a drum-tensioning device. Jamie Lee Curtis patented a nappy (diaper) with a pocket to hold disposable wipes. BTW, she is now Lady Haden-Guest through her marriage into a British aristocratic family. Danny Kaye invented a party toy that blew out three snakes when blown into.

HOLLYWOOD star Hedy Lamarr, glamour goddess of 1940s and 50s films, made mobile phones possible with their invention of Frequency-Hopping Spread Spectrum wireless. At the time, August 1942, she and her neighbour, avant garde composer George Atheil, invented it to make guided torpedo systems impossible for the enemy to interrupt (and despite the fact that both their families came from what was then enemy territory). At the time manufacturing couldn't cope with the idea, so Hedy was told to raise money for War Bonds instead (which she did, raising $7million on just one occasion). Later, when their patent had expired, it was realised the idea could make mobile phones possible.

GOOD CALL: Early mobile phones, often given nicknames such as 'the brick' because of their size and weight, had stubby little black aerials. They were pointless bits of rubber. The manufacturers thought buyers would expect an aerial, but the real one was inside the phone, as with later models.

LIFE SHAVINGS: Jacob Schick (born 1878) of Iowa, invented the electric razor because he believed that you could

extend your life expectancy to 120 years by shaving with great care. He patented the machine in 1923 but it was too big to be held in the hand. By 1927 he'd got it right and sold his first one in 1931, for $25 – then a lot of money. Within the first year he'd sold 3,000, but they all had to be 'kick started' by turning a small knurled wheel. But he didn't reach his age of 120, dying aged just 59 in 1937. Clean shaven.

NEW YORK theatre impresario Oscar Hammerstein, grandfather of the great 20th century lyricist with the same name, invented the cigar-rolling machine.

LIE DETECTORS AND WONDER WOMAN: William Moulton Marston who invented the lie detector test also created Wonder Woman, the cartoon character who later became a TV icon (above). In 1915 at the age of only 22 he had detected the systolic blood pressure test, and ways of measuring it, which led directly to the lie detector. It wasn't until 1941 that the first female superhero was launched on the comic-reading public. The character, you may recall, had a 'golden lasso of truth' that stopped people lying, among other powers.

MASS MARKET WASHING MACHINES: Came about because farmers won't buy things until they have to. Frederick Louis Maytag, born 1857, started a farm implement company in Newton, Iowa but couldn't get farmers to buy anything in certain seasons. The company began producing the Maytag washing machine in 1907 to give the workforce something to do.

DAFT ORIGINAL NAMES FOR THINGS WE NOW CALL ...

ASCENDING ROOMS – lifts or elevators
A DX-DY POSITION INDICATOR – computer mouse
SEPARABLE FASTENER – zipper or zip
HOOKLESS FASTENER – also zipper or zip
LOCKING TAPE – Velcro
HORSELESS CARRIAGE – car
OPTICAL ENGINE – telescope
ANALYTICAL ENGINE – computer (Babbage's mechanical one in the 19th century, but we today use 'search engine' so it's not so absurd)
DIFFERENCE ENGINE - calculator (below)
DRUNKOMETER – Breathalyser
MOVING STAIRCASE Escalator

The pocket calculator of its day: Babbage's difference engine

71

DISTAFF STUFF: Bulletproof vests, the circular saw and the bandsaw, fire escapes, windscreen wipers and laser printers were all invented by women.

FIRST PATENT in Britain was the ring binder invented in 1801 by the new Patent Office's chairman Dr Ayfor – suitable for filing patents No 2 onwards.

GOING OVERBOARD: Ole Evinrude, born 1877, was so annoyed at having to row a boat two miles across a lake to a picnic in 1906 that he invented the outboard motor.

APPLE COMPUTERS' LOGO: Is, some people claim, a tribute to a tragic brainbox's bizarre suicide. The logo shows an apple with a bite taken out of it. One bite out of a poisoned apple was, it is said, the method of death chosen by Alan Turing, the British computer genius who cracked the German Enigma code and thus hugely helped win World War II.

Turing had attended an English public school where he became aware of being homosexual. He had a tragic love affair with a fellow pupil who died young. After his war-winning code-breaking work - portrayed in the Robert Harris novel *Enigma* and by Benedict Cumberbatch and Keira Knightley in *The Imitation Game* - he ended up as an academic in Manchester but was exposed as a practising homosexual (then illegal) and threatened with prison. His reputation was ruined and his security clearance removed. He was found dead with, sources maintain, one bite taken out of a cyanide-laced apple. He had studied poisons for years.

It was ironic if he was pushed to take his own life when he had saved the lives of thousands - the sailors he had saved by using his code-breaking to defeat the U-boat menace in the

Battle of the Atlantic, and the hundreds of thousands more he saved by thus shortening the war.

Apple computers have never confirmed this origin, which seems to be urban myth, but a strange coincidence if it is. The bite could also refer to Eve and the Tree of Knowledge in the Garden of Eden. Or refer to the apple that fell on Newton's head. Or it could just be a simple joke on 'byte'. It's an enigma.

GREAT WRONG PREDICTIONS *No 3!*
President of the Royal Society, Lord Kelvin, in 1894 predicted that radio had no future. Now there are more than a billion radio sets tuned to 35,000 radio stations. He also said heavier-than-air flying machines would never work. Apart from that, he was spot on.

GREAT WRONG PREDICTIONS *No 4!*
Thomas Watson, the head of IBM, in 1943 forecast a world demand for possibly as many as five computers. Equally slow to see the market, Xerox was able to produce PCs in the 1970s, and did so for internal use, but decided to concentrate on making photocopiers as there was 'no further demand' for PCs.

WOODEN CREDIT IT: In the 1960s, Douglas Engelbart tried light pens and steering wheels before deciding on what we now call a mouse for use to guide the 'bug' on a computer screen. By bug, he meant what we now call the cursor. The first mouse was wood (pictured upside down), with two metal wheels which ran across a surface.

THINGS INVENTED LONG BEFORE THEY WERE NEEDED: or could be used, include the fax, 1843; the computer, 1834 (Charles Babbage's mechanical model); the on-ship aircraft landing in 1911; the first parachute jump in 1793 (from a balloon, more than 100 years before powered aircraft); contact lenses in 1888; bar codes in 1948; a helicopter, tank, solar power, double hull and calculator (well the concepts, not the products, by Da Vinci) 1470s; steam power by Hero in 50BC.

BRIGHT SPARK, EDISON: The electricity in your plug sockets is alternating current rather than direct current, decided only after a macabre process of testing it by cruelly killing conscious animals in public, and eventually a live human being in appalling agony.

This bizarre tale starts with Nikola Tesla walking through a Budapest park in 1881. He had suggested alternating current (where the current goes back and forth many times a second, as opposed to direct current which goes simply from positive to negative, as in a battery operated torch) as a student six years earlier but his professor had denounced the idea as claptrap.

Tesla watched the sun going down and thinking about the way the sun was still shining brightly further west on the planet, and that it would rise again in Budapest, with its field of light still around it causing a sunrise, and so realised spinning magnets could be arranged to create alternating current generators and drive AC motors. Arriving in America a few years later, Tesla tried to interest the famous Edison in AC electricity but was rebuffed. Tesla instead took out patents on AC in 1887 and convinced Edison's hated rival George Westinghouse to back the idea. BTW, the modern Tesla electric car is named after him.

KILLER EDISON: Edison was almost as incandescent with rage about Tesla (previous item) as were his light-bulbs. He set up bizarre demonstrations where dogs and cats were set

on sheets of metal and given 1,000 volts AC in front of invited guests and reporters. The idea was to show AC was far too dangerous to use, although as the animals convulsed, writhed and sparked in agony the effect may have been to put some people off electricity altogether and make them stick with gas lighting. Nevertheless, Edison's men used larger animals in the sick demonstrations. 'Is this what your wife should be cooking with?' they would demand from the audience as the animals died writhing in agony before them. Never mind the fact that householders using DC were finding out that with this, too, touching 'live' terminals meant death.

Edison (above) then astounded everyone by taking out a licence to use the hated rival AC. Why? It turned out that he'd done a deal with a New York prison and created the first electric chair. An unfortunate William Kemmler was selected as the first to use it on August 6, 1890. 'Come and see a man be Westinghoused', Edison's frankly crude propaganda went. In fact poor Kemmler didn't die straight away, although he convulsed and there was a repulsive smell of charred flesh. The voltage (700) and amperage wasn't enough with only two electrodes, one on his head and one on his spine. He had to be given a second dose (of 1,030 volts) as his suffering went on – which probably delighted Edison as the more gruesome a death by AC, the better. It was not until two minutes into the second dose that Kemmler went limp.

OLD SPARKY: Meanwhile the electric chair, sometimes dubbed

Old Sparky (below), came into widespread use across America, despite its terrible failure to kill Kemmler quickly. A proper hangman would have been a lot quicker, cheaper, more reliable and more humane. It may be that as the electrodes were improved, they gave the impression of giving a quick and painless death because the victim was paralysed and hooded. There have certainly been cases of more than one shock being necessary.

BATTERIES NOT INCLUDED: An African chief who heard about electric chairs was impressed and ordered three. As his country didn't have any electricity, they didn't work, so he made one into his throne. Likewise the artist Andy Warhol who bought one previously used at San Quentin prison didn't turn the power on but sat in it to watch horror films. Nice.

EDISON WRONG: Edison, whom we were all taught to admire at school, not only didn't invent many of the inventions he has been credited with, not only used the agonising deaths of others to promote his selfish ends (previous items), but he was also totally wrong on the science.

His preferred system DC isn't less dangerous than AC but it is far less efficient over any distance. Consider electrified railways. The lines south of London are electrified by Edison's

DC. A whole extra railway line – the insulated third rail – is run beside the tracks and where this breaks, for a crossing for example, you can see the massive cable needed to convey enough current at 750v DC is about as thick as a man's lower leg. Substations need to be every few miles because the current cannot be transmitted further. North of London, on the other hand, the lines are powered by Westinghouse's alternating current. The cable (suspended over the tracks) is only about as thick as your thumb (at 25,000v AC) and yet the trains can go much faster than their southern rivals. And the substations can be 40 miles apart. Proof that Edison wasn't such a live wire. On very high voltages, however, it may be different.

STINK JET? Before Hewlett and Packard got it together with computers and printers, they invented an automatic urinal flusher. And no need to buy pesky refill cartridges.

GREAT WRONG PREDICTIONS *No 5!*
In 1899 the director of the U.S. Patent Office told President McKinley that his job was a waste of time because 'everything that can be invented has already been invented'.

PAINLESS AND STAINLESS: Harry Brearly was trying to make better rifle barrels in Sheffield, England in 1913 when he noticed that his new mixture, with added chromium, didn't rust. He'd accidentally created stainless steel, with a host of peaceful uses.

MICROWAVE ovens were invented in 1946 when Dr Percy Spencer was working on radar and noticed the chocolate in his pocket had melted. The first Radarange oven stood 6ft tall and cost more than $5,000.

THINGS going unexpectedly hard, on the other hand, was what happened with experimental drug UK92480, supposed to be a treatment for angina, where heart blood supply is constricted. It didn't work very well, but male volunteers trialling it found they were having sustained erections.

Result: Pfizer had one of the most profitable drugs ever created – Viagra, a treatment for erectile dysfunction.

BARBIE CUE: Jack Ryan who helped perfect the Barbie doll for the giant Mattel toy corporation, had previously worked for the Department of Defense creating lethal missiles. Launched in 1958, she was the first doll with adult features – before that, people assumed little girls wanted to play with dolls of little girls. In fact they wanted to fantasise about being grown up, albeit in a rather strange shape. Like the missiles, the doll was bang on target. The detailed designers Ruth and Elliot Handler named her after their daughter Barbara. BTW, Ryan was briefly the sixth husband of Zsa Zsa Gabor, and when their marriage hit the rocks, he took her Rolls-Royce to pieces and refused to reassemble it. BTW (2), Jack Ryan's name was used by Tom Clancy for his CIA hero, later portrayed by Harrison Ford.

PIGEON POO led to the discovery of the biggest event in the entire universe. In 1964 American scientists Arno Penzias and Robert Wilson were annoyed at the background hiss while they were studying radio emissions from the Milky Way. They suspected interference was caused by roosting pigeons dropping their excrement on their antenna, so they went up and cleaned it. The hissing continued. It was the echoes of the Big Bang that created every atom in this book and the person holding it and the planet around you. They won the 1978 Nobel Prize for it. The pigeons also got a big

bang – they were shot. The term 'big bang', BTW, was coined by astronomers who didn't believe it, in ridicule. What, you think it all started with some kind of *Big Bang*?

SPANGLERING: By rights you should Spangler the carpet after a party, not Hoover it. The inventor of the electric vacuum cleaner was an American boffin, Murray Spangler; William H. Hoover was merely the canny businessman who recognised a great sucker - literally - when he saw one, and really cleaned up. Early vacuum cleaners had been horse-drawn appliances that visited your house and had a great long tube snaking in the front door to suck out dust.

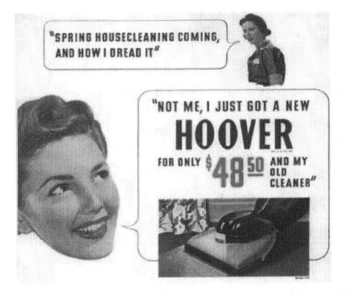

LATER British inventor James Dyson saw the way industrial dust extractors used centrifugal force and came up with the bagless vacuum cleaner. Fears that his marketing slogan 'Ditch the bag' could be taken the wrong way by housewives were groundless, but then rival Electrolux tried the even more cheeky 'Nothing sucks like an Electrolux'. Old Spangler (above) didn't know what he'd started. Perhaps his view would be a philosophical 'So long, suckers.'

SCIENCE knows pretty well everything, and explains everything, doesn't it? Whatever Newton didn't sort out, Einstein is supposed to have nailed down: and science is true because you can repeat anything in experiments. Well, no, and *that's* the biggest secret about science. You're sitting on a chair reading this, probably. What force is keeping you on that chair despite the planet spinning through space at vast speed? Gravity. At the time of writing, nobody knows what that most basic force gravity is: is it gravity waves, or particles called gravitons? And no one knows exactly how and why life was first created. We're just told that if you shook up a load of primeval mud in a test tube for long enough you'd get butterflies, begonias and Bach or dinosaurs, dragonflies and Danny DeVito.

So why can't they repeat it, even to one amoeba? No one knows what most of the universe – the so-called dark matter – is made of or how to detect it. No one knows how big the Universe is or even what shape it is or what was here before, or after, or why. No one knows what time is made of, yet it can be bent, so it must be something. They have theories about some of these things, but nothing that can be replicated in experiments. And no one knows in detail how the human brain works. Where is personality, the ego, the id, the soul, where *exactly* are these words that you are reading stored in your head? Could a surgeon find that one word exactly or reconstruct it from the grey matter? Not a chance. Apart from that, yes, science has got all the answers...

AND for a little fun to fill in this page, places where things *should* have been invented but, sadly, weren't. Bicycle bell: Tring, Hertfordshire, Rubber band: Penang, Malaysia. Trampoline: Dordogne, France. Ice cream dispenser: Splott, a suburb of Cardiff. Catapult: Pyongyang, North Korea. Garden fork: Krong, Norway. Viagra: Pill, Newport, Wales.

7 Cars, traffic and planes: Funniest facts about your transport

PULP FRICTION: Pulped paperbacks are mixed with tar used in British road-making to produce a more noise absorbent surface. 'We prefer romantic fiction because it's softer,' said a spokesman. Seriously. The A1 not far from Barbara Cartland's Hertfordshire home was paved with Mills & Boon – publishers of the type of novel of which wrote a record 723.

FORD GOAT DUNG: The name suggested for the Ford Capri was originally Ford Capino, until it was realised this was Italian slang for goat dung.

MAKING HIS MERC IN HISTORY: A U.S. celebrity who named his daughter Mercedes recently was soundly mocked by media chatterers for using a posh car name for a girl. One commentator on a website said: 'Who names their daughter Mercedes? What next? Ferrari? McLaren? Lamborghini?'

But it is the sneerers who should be mocked: it was the other way round. Mercedes was and is a perfectly good girl's name. In 1899 Emil Jellinek was racing Benz cars when he decided to name his team Mercedes after his daughter. The name stuck because the team kept winning, and became the car brand.

What *was* odd was that it was so successful that the father changed his name to Jellinek-Mercedes, saying it was the first time a father had ever taken his daughter's name. The father was known as 'that mad Englishman' because he would ride around Nice and Vienna on as penny-farthing bicycle wearing a safari helmet and plus fours, but he wasn't an Englishman, he merely behaved like one. At the age of 17, he had been sacked by a railway company for organising secret train races late at night.

Not something you can easily keep quiet – two steam trains hurtling down parallel tracks. His daughter Mercedes wasn't ever interested in cars, named after her or not, and died in 1929.

THE WALRUS-BENZ: The man who created and marketed the Mercedes brand wasn't as pleased with the cars as may be thought. Some of Jellinek's telegrams to the manufacturers:
"You are all donkeys"
"Your manure wagon has just broken down on schedule"
"Your third-rate factory"
"Your engineers should be locked up in an insane asylum"
"Your car is a cocoon and I want the butterfly"
Teams that could have become household names for posh cars had Mercedes not won in the 1899 races included: Dr. Pascal, Axt, Escargot and Walrus. If Mercedes seems a small mercy in comparison, the word means mercies in Spanish.

GRAND PRIX GIRLS: Other girls apparently named after motor cars included Megane Renault in Belgium (they are both in fact legitimate names for a person) and Elise Lotus in Britain.

VOLVO: Means I roll in Latin because it was a ball-bearing factory to start with.

AFFORD A FORD: Wouldn't you love it if car prices were a third of what they were 20 years ago? In 1908, the Model T Ford was introduced at $825. Because of mass production, by 1925 the price was only $260. Ford is credited with inventing mass production. He didn't. Marc Isambard Brunel did a century earlier at Portsmouth Dockyard, England, making pulley blocks for the Royal Navy. To fight the French. Which he was, BTW.

POACHED EGG CARS: The first great British postwar success for Morris cars, the Morris Minor, was produced *despite* the factory's founder William Morris (Lord Nuffield). He saw the jelly-mould like design - built by his design team in secret away from his gaze - and he sneeringly called it 'a poached egg'. In fact it had been a taller, narrower prototype but brilliant designer Alec Issigonis could see the look was wrong. He had the first car sawn in half from front to back and moved apart until there was a two-inch gap and then said: 'That's it. Make them that wide.' The Morris Minor (below) sold millions up until the 1970s.

BUZZ: The cars should have been called the Morris Mosquito, but in the end the pre-war Morris Minor name was re-used, perhaps suiting the austerity and modesty of the era. The much-appreciated ample room in the engine bay, which made amateur repairs so easy, was an accident. One, because the car was sawn in half and widened (pictured above), two because Issigonis wanted a flat-four-cylinder engine which would have needed more space, but in the event the money men couldn't spare the cash to develop one.

MINI MIRACLE: In 1959 Issigonis took the same four-cylinder engine and turned it sideways to make the Mini,

(pictured below) with front-wheel drive, which was very much more compact and a massive hit through the next three decades, starring in the film The Italian Job. But he forgot when he did so that the distributor (which delivers the power to the spark plugs) would then end up at the front of the car. Thus early Minis when driven through even fairly shallow puddles would often stop and have to be dried out. The modern Mini, built in the same Oxford factory but by BMW, avoids this problem.

BANNED BMW: The superior German car brand BMW, that now owns Rolls-Royce and Mini in Britain, got into motor manufacturing only because it was banned from making aircraft engines after Germany lost World War I. Its logo shows a stylised turning propeller for that reason. The first car it produced was a British Austin 7 under licence, but BMW's quality eventually far exceeded Austin's and BMW outsold and outlived that company.

HITLER'S TRICK: Volkswagen, the people's car literally, was sold as a concept to the Germans by Hitler, who failed to deliver the cars they were paying for, spending the money on the war instead. The man who *did* ensure they got the VW Beetles was, ironically, a British Army officer. Major Ivan Hirst looked at the bombed out factory in 1945 and realised if ruined Germany was to have any future, people must get back to work. He persuaded the British military to order 20,000 cars and this got the factory going again, this time producing the little cars the Germans had been promised and not military vehicles. *Any* future? Some 15,000,000 Beetles and 27 years later, it became the best-selling car of all time, also outliving British rivals.

HITLER AND FORD: Adolf Hitler had a framed photo of Henry Ford on his office wall. Ford was the only American mentioned in his book *Mein Kampf.* Ford may have done more than most people for the American consumer and worker, but for a while dallied with owning antisemitic publications, until he recanted and apologised in 1927. Even after that, Hitler's consul at Cleveland gave Ford the Grand Cross of the German Eagle, Hitler's highest honour, festooned with four swastikas.

FORD AND EDISON: Ford admired Thomas Edison, for whom he worked early in his career, and on the latter's deathbed insisted his son held up a test tube to catch his last breath, which is on display in the Henry Ford museum.

GREAT WRONG PREDICTIONS *No 6!*
In the early 20th century it was estimated that the world market could only be 4 million automobiles because 'the world would run out of chauffeurs'.

EXPLODING TRAFFIC LIGHTS: The world's first traffic lights were installed in 1868 before motor vehicles had been introduced in Bridge Street, Westminster to ease the immense horse-drawn traffic. The gas powered lights, which had semaphore arms as well as lights, being designed by railway engineer Saxby, later exploded, killing the policeman operating them.

GAS-POWERED street lights started in Pall Mall, London in 1807, using barrels of old muskets as (dangerously leaky) pipes. But one lamp outside the Savoy Hotel extracted the explosive methane from the sewer below and burnt that. It was lit by posh people's poo. Oddly London still has 1,500 gas lamps and five lamplighters. As the mechanisms are now clockwork, they don't in fact light the lamps but do maintain and clean them. Some people notice that there are some streets still with gas lights only during electric power cuts.

HIGH ROLLER: The lettering (below) on the top of the distinguished radiators of Roll-Royce cars was turned black from the original red on the death of Henry Royce in 1933. Charles Rolls, his partner who had been issued with British pilot's licence No 2 in 1910, had been killed in that same year in his aircraft. Oddly, given that his name is now associated with luxury, Rolls used to sleep under his cars to avoid paying hotel bills.

SS CARS: Jaguar cars should be called SS cars. They were until the end of the Second World War when it was considered the name SS – derived from Swallow Sidecars, the original 1921 company – sounded rather like staff cars for Himmler and his German *Schutzstaffeln* shock troops. Not a logo (the infamous one below) you would like on your car.

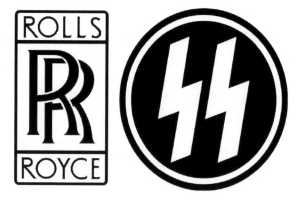

AMBLER GAMBLERS: The first British automatic traffic lights were installed in Wolverhampton in 1927, and powered by clockwork, but that town insisted they should go straight from red to green (as do many Continental ones today), because it was concerned about the dangers of

'amber gamblers'. Eventually it was forced to comply with national norms.

OFFICER POTTS'S BRIGHT IDEA: The first American traffic lights were invented by Police Officer William Potts who used electric railway signals. They were installed in 1919 in Detroit, Michigan. A man had to operate them, so they could possibly be green in all directions. The USA's first automatic traffic light was in Houston, Texas, or rivals claim, Cleveland, Ohio.

HEAD-ON: Ohio was good for automobile firsts. It produced the first American gas-powered (petrol-driven, that is) car in 1891, built by John William Lambert, and the first accident when it crashed later that year. The way motor traffic was going to go was perhaps suggested by Mississippi in the year when there were just two cars in all the roads of that vast state. They crashed head on.

A DASHBOARD was fixed to the front of carriages so mud *dashed* up by horses' hooves didn't spatter passengers. The term was extended to the similarly angled board separating the engine from passengers in cars.

LIMOUSINE cars and the Limousin breed of cattle have something in common – they relate to the Limousin region of France. Indirectly, in the case of the car, whose all-over roof enveloping the passengers in total privacy reminded someone of a Limousin cloak.

GERMAN ENGINEER August Horch's name meant listen, as in 'hark!' In English. So Horch (1868-1951, pictured below) called his firm the same thing in Latin – Audi.

CADILLAC ARREST: In the USA, car brands are strangely intertwined. Buick employed Louis Chevrolet, Cadillac (example above) was formed from the remnants of the Henry Ford Company after Ford left to start the Ford Motor Company, and Walter Chrysler was also employed by Buick. Oldsmobiles originally had Dodge engines.

WHILE British car-making tycoon William Morris started out making bicycles in Oxford, Clement Studebaker's blacksmith firm in South Bend, Indiana started making wagons for settlers heading west, then wheelbarrows for the gold rush and U.S. Army wagons for the Civil War before eventually trying motorised vehicles, creating the famed Studebaker marque. BTW, Clement is the patron saint of blacksmiths.

FRIPPERIES: Chrysler became the first car maker to offer headlamps included in the standard price: meanwhile British manufacturers in the 1920s thought brakes on all four wheels would make drivers careless and resisted such fripperies. Later, the designer of the Morris Mini thought radios, comfortable seats, wind-up windows etc were not wanted, and early models didn't have these.

WHOSE fault was it that competitive Japanese motorcycles

squashed many Western makes and severely damaged others such as Harley-Davidson? Er, Harley-Davidson, who sold blueprints, machinery, dies and tools to the Sankyo Company of Japan in 1935, causing the first Japanese motorbikes to be made. (Mind you, we Brits shouldn't mock too much. Who taught the Japanese to fly planes off ships between the wars? Er, the Royal Navy.)

Please don't read the next three paragraphs if you're offended by rude stuff. This not only gets us out of trouble but also ensures you read every word.

THE OPEN RUDE: Car model names can translate badly. The Toyota MR2 read out in French quickly says Toyota Shit. The Vauxhall Nova in Spanish-speaking countries if read as three words would mean Vauxhall Doesn't Go. The Ford Focus in parts of Ireland sounds like Ford Fuck Us.

IT GETS WORSE: Mitsubishi had a horse-related theme in the 1990s in model names such as the Colt and Lancer. When they brought out a Starion, wags in the West claimed that they were trying to say Stallion. The firm then tried to play it safe with Pajero, although in some Spanish countries it means Masturbator. The Buick LaCrosse when exported to Quebec seemed to be Buick Wanker. The Ford Pinto meant the Ford Prick in Brazilian slang. Ford, to be fair, quickly realised this and used another name. Either way, the silly name was the least of problems for a car famous for exploding petrol tanks.

AND WORSE: The Honda Fitta was rapidly changed to Honda Jazz when it was discovered it was slang for female genitalia in Sweden. Which is what the Opel Ascona meant in Portugal and Galicia. While the Mazda Laputa meant the Mazda Whore to some South Americans. And Roll-Royce Silver Mist meant Roll-Royce Silver Horseshit in German slang. Tough Mist, boys.

AND FUNNY: Car names that were just laughable, not rude: For inappropriateness - Hillman Avenger (for a car that,

frankly, had all the sexy acceleration of a wet lettuce), Wolseley Hornet (a too buzzy name for a sad and feeble Mini clone). For pretension - Chrysler Imperial LeBaron, or The Ford Country Squire. For unattractiveness - The Dodge Ram Miser, and the Studebaker Dictator, produced just in time for the rise of Mussolini and Hitler. It was marketed as the Director in the countries affected. When Hitler got too notorious, the name was changed to the Commander.

JAPANESE CAR NAMES: Tend to be the firm's name and a seemingly appropriate English word. But they aren't always appropriate: Toyota Stout, Mazda Scrum, Daihatsu Naked, Honda Joy Machine.

THE WORLD'S MOST EXPENSIVE TYRE (OR TIRE) costs $25,000, is 13ft tall and weighs as much as eight small cars. It fits only the Caterpillar 797B dump truck, which is used in mining and carries 380 tonnes of rock with a 117.1 Litre turbocharged diesel engine producing 3,550 horsepower. The truck is nearly 50ft long and weighs 278 tons empty. Not easy to park in a multi-storey…

GETTING THE BENDS: The Rotherhithe road tunnel under the Thames has two bends in it so a horse wouldn't see the light at the end of the tunnel and bolt to get out.

PARISIAN MAYHEM: French car insurance policies sometimes exclude the Place de l'Etoile, around the Arc de Triomphe in Paris, where 12 roads meet in an unregulated roundabout (below) and total mayhem ensues daily.

KEEP WHAT? In only one road in Britain is it correct to drive on the right – Savoy Court, the road leading to the Savoy Hotel, London, off the Strand.

DAGGER DANGER: Driving on the left in Britain originates from the need to keep the right hand facing the oncoming horse rider, for greeting, or drawing a sword or dagger.

ROMAN LEFTIES: The Romans in Britain also drove on the left. This can be seen from a quarry in Wiltshire where uncovered wheel ruts showed the loaded wagons keeping to the left, the lighter returning ones on the other side.

BILL OF RIGHTS: In the United States it was common for wagons to be drawn by four horses controlled by a man riding one (unlike in Britain where the driver sat on the cart, and most carts had only one or two horses). To use the whip effectively on all four horses with his right hand he had to sit on the rear left horse. To watch his wheels didn't hit passing vehicles from this position he therefore needed to pass them on his left, ie drive on the right. Plus it annoyed the Brits who thought they knew best, a useful side benefit.

IT HAD TO HAPPEN. On August 17, 1896, the first Briton was killed by a motor car. The Anglo-French Motorcar Corporation was demonstrating its horseless carriages in the grounds of the Crystal Palace, in South London, when Mrs Bridget Driscoll walked in front of a machine driven by Arthur Edsel. At the inquest, the driver insisted that he been driving at the prescribed 4mph. Although there were warning signs, no one had yet decided on which side of the road cars should drive. The Coroner said 'We must make sure that this never happens again'. Since then, it has happened again 450,000 times – the number of Britons slain by British motorists. That's 100,000 more than the combined forces of Hitler, Mussolini and Hirohito managed in World War II.

BLUE RAYS: Blue lights on British emergency vehicles may be used by many more services than the assumed three: over a dozen. Among the unusual ones are: Human Transplant vehicles, Naval Nuclear Monitoring, Forestry Commission Fire Service, Mine Rescue, and Mountain Rescue.

BLUES AND TWOS: The two-tone sirens and blue lights are known by British police as 'Blues and twos'. The traffic police cars are known as Jam Sandwiches because of the red stripe on a white background. Or Battenbergs where they are in large chequered pattern. The black and white ones were Panda cars.

COPPING IT: One of the most dangerous things on British roads is the police. In the year to April 2004, 2,000 people were injured and 31 killed by emergency services on 999 calls. Among famous victims of this type of accident was Heather Mills (later McCartney), who lost part of her leg to a police motorcyclist in Kensington High Street.

PADDY AND MARIA: Police vans are called Paddy Wagons in the USA (for no known reason, except that the cops and/or the criminals may have been Irish) and Black Marias in Britain (pictured) and several other countries (again for no known reason). Given that its origin is obscure, it's odd that the name Black Maria was also used for an American locomotive, a First World War Canadian fighter ace's aircraft, a Vietnam War CIA helicopter, a cartoon collection, a card game, two novels, two film festivals, a pub, a cartoon company, a film studio, two rock bands, two songs and an album, and is included in the lyrics of five more songs. Still no one knew what it meant. And the Black Marias weren't even black, but usually dark blue.

LEAD was added to petrol to enable high performance without 'pinking' in the cylinders, but it meant that children living near busy roads were showered with poison which was known to produce mental impairment. No one knows for sure what the damage was, but it's a fact that the otherwise inexplicable reduction in crime – particularly low level stuff like vandalism, street violence and petty theft – happened exactly in line with the reduction in lead levels.

FLIGHT FRIGHT: If all the flights heading for the Eastern United States arrived on time, the airports couldn't cope. A certain amount of chaos allows them to function. If all the airliners in the world were on the ground at once, there wouldn't be nearly enough terminal gates.

IN THE AIR: At any one time 366,144 people are in the air on aircraft worldwide, on average. The number of passengers in the air above London at any moment is 1,875 (averages calculated in 2001). Meanwhile 450,000 people are cruising at an altitude of minus 20ft to minus 100ft in the London rush hour, in 460 moving Tube trains.

SO LONG, SUCKERS: For a jumbo jet to take off, the engines must suck in the amount of air equivalent to four squash courts every second.

PISTON-POWERED SHOES: In post-Soviet Russia, inventor Roman Kunikov came up with petrol (gas) powered boots that put a bang in your stride, so you can take 12ft steps (about 4 metres). Pistons were strapped to each calf and every time your foot came down, a bang in them forced down a metal plate under the heel, hurling the wearer upwards a foot or two. Skilled wearers could easily reach 25mph (40kmh). The boots contain a small petrol tank, a carburettor and a spark plug mechanism, plus springs for absorbing the shock of landing. You just adjust the

carburettor according to your weight, and step on the gas. Kunikov was quoted as saying the design would be continually improved. 'We aren't going to stay standing in one place.' Not if they're turned on they won't.

THE British owner of the company making the Segway, an unlikely-looking self balancing two-wheel transport, died on one, when he and it fell over a cliff in 2010.

HOT BETWEEN THE LEGS? The Science Museum in London has a steam-powered motorcycle which necessitated riding with a coal brazier between your knees. Not bad on an icy day, but perhaps uncomfortable in a mid-summer traffic jam. But you could have roast nuts at any time.

HURRY CURRY: In 2005 it was revealed that an Australian had managed to power a moped with gas (fart, not gasoline) from his colostomy bag. He had noticed that his guts produced enormous amounts of methane and hooked it up to the carburettor of a very small motor. It actually worked for short distances, and considerably reduced the smell.

PIG SAVINGS: Meanwhile a South African farmer with a pig manure surplus found that if you put the porkers' poo in a large open-topped oil drum, then put another slightly smaller drum upside down in the first, the gas would collect in the top drum, which would rise slowly. A hose in the top would collect the pongy product which was compressed into cylinders and ran all his cars successfully. The smell was absolutely appalling, however – particularly when he left the home-made gas holders too long once and they exploded. But if you did it right, you ended up with a manure that could be composted with straw and used as excellent fertiliser. But not many friends, possibly.

FRYING SQUAD: And in Britain, less disgusting smells were emanating from old diesel car owners who found that their vehicles would run perfectly well on old cooking oil. This they could get free from pubs and chip shops who otherwise would have to pay to have it taken away. The only problem was that it was illegal, unless you paid the Government 47p duty per litre. The police would become suspicious if they were following a car that left a scent of scampi and chips, or cod in batter, as they do. The unit that could confiscate the cars and fine the owners was nicknamed the Frying Squad.

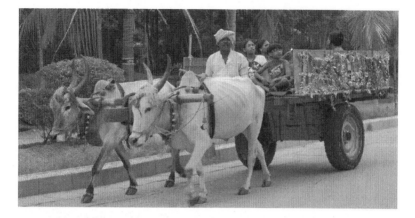

JUMPING BULLOCKS: In Jaipur, Rajasthan, India, under a 2007 law, you must obtain a licence from the city council before driving a bullock cart through the town. To get this you must be free of infectious diseases: there is also provision for a 100 rupee fine for a bullock cart – notoriously heavily laden and slow – jumping a red light. *Jumping?*

A BOEING 747-400 has six million parts (including every last rivet and screw), 147 miles of wiring and a wingspan about twice as long as the Wright Brothers' first flight.

THE VW model called Phaeton recalls what classical allusion? Something elegant and refined? No. It's the story of a psychopathically reckless teenager whose driving almost destroys the entire world and has to be shot dead. Phaeton was the arrogant son of Apollo and he borrowed Dad's chariot – the one that tows the sun across the sky every day. His reckless driving threatened to crash the sun into the world, killing everyone. Apollo had no choice but to fire a

lightning bolt at his son, killing him. Still, VW Apocalypse-Kill-Psycho-Teen just wouldn't sound quite right, would it?

AA roadside rescue vans in Britain are bright yellow (below) for safety reasons, right? No. One of the founders of the Automobile Association was eccentric – not to say barking – aristocrat the 5th Earl of Lonsdale, known as the 'Yellow Earl' because of his obsession with the colour. He wanted his houses, waistcoats, servants, everything painted yellow, so the AA had to adopt the colour. He wasted a vast fortune, somehow managing to spend £100,000 a year on cigars over 100 years ago, and entertained kings and an emperor royally at his family seat Lowther Castle in Cumbria, which he lost through extravagance. He did, however, start many things – the Lonsdale Belt in boxing, for example. And the AA. The patrolmen on the earlier motorbikes (below), used to salute passing AA members. Difficult!

8 Trains and canals: How our ancestors went absolutely loco

THE HORSE BUM LINE: The standard gauge of railways worldwide – the 4ft 8½in between the tracks – which was settled after a huge battle in Britain in the 19th century and subsequently used in most countries – was really decided by a horse's bum long before Christ was born. George Stephenson, who built the first proper railway in 1825, wanted his tracks to take the existing horse-drawn rail wagons from mine workings. Their width was decided by how wide the shafts have to be for a horse to fit between them. This must have applied since the first horse-drawn wagon was created.

If you don't believe it, check the distance between Roman chariot wheels. They are pretty close to 4ft 8½in and, with flanges on, some of them could have run down the Piccadilly line in the London Underground to the British Museum, or any other standard gauge railway around the world. What was thought to be an early Greek standard gauge railway by excited archaeologists turned out to be stone wagonways with the ruts worn into a very regular groove, again at around 4ft 8½in spacing. The first man to make a decent chariot in ancient Sumeria or wherever in effect decided the track gauge of France's TGV today.

KEEP YOUR AIR ON: Just about every train in the world, and most lorries and buses, are stopped by air brakes, which are safer than hydraulic brakes. However this was the reaction of American railway tycoon **Cornelius Vanderbilt** to George Westinghouse's invention in 1869: 'Do you pretend to tell me you could stop a train with *wind*? I'll give you to understand, young man, that I am too busy to have any time taken up talking to a damned fool.'

TRAINS suffer from flat tyres too. The outer part of the wheel is a shrunk-on steel tyre and if this develops a flat through heavy braking with a locked wheel, the vehicle rolls with a bang-bang-bang-bang which is bad for the track - and annoying for passengers.

FIT AN MP CATCHER: The world's first cowcatcher (the sloping thing on the front of railway trains, above, that in movies scoops bison out of the way in the Wild West) was designed, logically enough, by the man who saw the world's first fatal railway accident. However, it wasn't in Vulture Gulch, Arkansas but in Newton-le-Willows, Merseyside, where MP William Huskisson was run down by Stephenson's *Rocket* because he crossed a track on the Liverpool & Manchester railway's opening day in 1830. George Stephenson himself drove Huskisson rapidly to Eccles on the train but he died there a few hours later. Witnessing this was Sir George Cayley MP, who designed the first cowcatcher for the front of locomotives. They never caught on in Britain, but with the unfenced railways of the USA were much used there. BTW, Cayley also designed and built an aircraft, and an engine that ran on gunpowder.

THE real reason Huskisson died (previous item) is even more curious. Stephenson had an odd idea that with a pair of tracks, if the space between them was just right, a train could run up the middle if needed. To us this seems bonkers – how would the train be switched over to balance on those two inner rails? Surely it would block both proper tracks? But this was early days, and steel rails were not available, just fragile iron ones. The result was that the now customary wider gap between the tracks wasn't there, and Huskisson couldn't stand aside in what railwaymen now call the 'six foot' between the closest rails of a pair of railway lines. It wasn't 6ft at all, it was exactly 4ft 8½in.

RED BOTTOM: 'Traffic lights' for trains – that is electric light signals – have the red light at the bottom so that snow cannot build up on the hood of a light underneath and obscure that most important signal. On British high speed rail routes there are four lights, so the first warning can be double yellow, the brightest possible. These two, separated by the green to make it clearer, can be seen up to four miles away in the right conditions.

COLOUR-BLIND: Road drivers can judge traffic lights by their positions; colour-blind train drivers are illegal and candidates are tested to detect this.

THE RIGHT ATMOSPHERE: Crackpot railway ideas abounded from the earliest days. The great engineer Brunel thought having a train pulled by a piston sucked along a vacuum pipe would avoid having a locomotive and installed his 'atmospheric railway' in Starcross, Devon – despite locals ridiculing what they thought would be a train flying through the atmosphere. There was the problem of joining the piston to the carriages, which was done through a slot covered in a greased leather flap. Surprisingly, it worked very well for a short while, but then rats ate the leather, causing leaks, and sun and sea air caused further deterioration. And the men greasing the flaps were run down because the trains were silent. It was soon abandoned as steam locos improved.

THIS SUCKS: Another inventor in New York made a subway vacuum train with the whole carriage fitting tightly in the tunnel so it could be sucked along. It worked too, but passengers were in agony as their eardrums burst.

BIT OF A BLOW: Another crackpot scheme that was built against all common sense involved blowing rather than sucking trains. George Bennie's 1930s railplane (above), a cigar-shaped carriage with aircraft propellers fore and aft was supposed to run suspended from an impossibly complicated gantry above existing railway lines. The ordinary track was supposed to carry heavy goods, while railplanes sped passengers and mail at 300mph. Bennie paid for a demonstration line at Milngarvie, near Glasgow, which opened in July 1930. The machine never reached anything like the predicted speeds, despite the great noise of thrashing the air, and World War II put paid to Bennie's dreams. Oddly, the massive rig survived until early 1956. George Bennie died the following year, aged 65, having never recovered from the blow.

IRISH INGENUITY: In the search for economies, at least two railways laid only one rail instead of the usual pair – a sort of monorail. One in India, had special engines and carriages with most of the weight carried on the one rail and a strange outrigger road wheel bouncing along the highway alongside. It tended to fall over. More successful was the Irish one that had one rail at waist height on a series of A-frames and carriages, trucks and locos that hung down both sides like cycle panniers. It was called the Lartigue system (above). Loads had to be balanced, which was tackled with Irish ingenuity.

When a cow was sent to market, two calves were sent in the other side. The calves could then go one each side on the way back. The Listowel & Ballybunion (honestly!) Railway opened in 1888, and a working replica has recently been installed for tourists in County Kerry. As you can imagine, the points and turntables (previous page) are very strange, and as for level crossings, forget it.

SAILWAY TRAIN: It was in Ireland, too, that the sailing train was discovered. Setting a sail on a railway truck in the Atlantic winds would power it for miles. The trouble was, you couldn't tack upwind on the way back (well not unless the tracks zigzagged!), so all the trucks ended up at one end of the line unless the wind reversed. The idea was copied by the Newtyle & Coupar Angus Railway in Scotland, which extended it to passenger workings. A sail-driven coach was followed by a horse, however, in case the wind dropped. Or perhaps for bringing it back.

ICE LOCOMOTIVE: It sounds like something Roald Dahl or C.S. Lewis would have made up, but it was real. In Russia ice locomotives (below) were used on frozen rivers and lakes to avoid the cost of railway tracks and bridges. Not surprisingly, they weren't as heavy as regular express engines, and featured spikes on the main driving wheels and sledge-like runners (steerable by chains) where the front four small wheels would be on a normal locomotive. They would pull a carriage or wagons, also on sleds.

Ry. & Loco. Eng.

FIG. 31. GREW'S ICE LOCOMOTIVE FOR RUSSIA, 1861.

ICE RAILWAY: If that seems unlikely, recall that during the terrible siege of Leningrad in the 1940s, a life-saving road and then a whole full-sized railway were built across the frozen Lake Lagoda to supply the city. It was even equipped with anti-aircraft guns along the track to deter German bombers from blowing holes in the ice. Nor was this the first such lake railway.

In 1904 during Russia's war with Japan, Moscow needed to move troops rapidly across Siberia. Normally, the several-hundred-mile-long Lake Baikal, which was then a gap in the Trans-Siberian Railway, was crossed by British-built ice-breaking rail ferries, previously assembled on its shores from a kit of parts. But to speed things up in 1904, the Russians laid tracks directly on the frozen lake. It worked for a while, until locomotives broke through the ice...

FLOATING TRAIN: An even more bizarre wartime expedient was a German floating freight train towed by ships. In 1944, when Germany was losing World War II, its armed forces were desperately short of fuel because of allied bombing of supply facilities. Seventy highly useful rail tank cars were cut off by the Russians in the port of Memel. A German engineering officer calculated that the 25-ton tank wagons would float if sealed and thus by night bizarre convoys of coupled wagons were towed across the Baltic to Pillau, west of Koenigsberg, an area still held by the Germans. A few days later a Luftwaffe plane was sent up to attack a submarine that was menacing coastal shipping. It turned out that the 'submarine' was a tank wagon that had broken away from the strange floating train. A tug was sent out and retrieved it.

FORGOTTEN TUBE STATIONS: London not only has the world's biggest Tube network but also more disused Underground stations and lines than most cities have on their entire network – an amazing 48 where only ghost trains call. Some of these were little more than above-ground halts that later closed or moved, or stations on the annoyingly-cluttered Piccadilly Line, which has, thankfully for passengers heading for Heathrow, lost Brompton Road and Down Street in Central London plus six other suburban stations.

OTHER GHOST STATIONS are on sections of London Underground line completely abandoned, the first and oldest being King William Street in the City. The City and South London Railway, the world's first electrically-operated Tube, opened from Stockwell in South London in 1890. Because of Parliament's insistence that the newfangled Tube should not burrow beneath buildings, even in the tightly-packed City, the King William Street terminus was badly laid out with the approach so steep and twisting that trains sometimes had to have several runs at it, and there was poor access for passengers too. Nevertheless, such was the success of the railway that an extension to Moorgate (now the City branch of the Northern Line) was opened from Borough in 1900, leaving 1,267 yards of former track to King William Street disused for more than a century (and reopened as a bomb shelter in both world wars). Other whole branches lost include the Aldwych Line and the Charing Cross end of the Jubilee Line, which was diverted elsewhere in 1999.

CRAVEN NONSENSE: Until 2007, Eurostar trains did London Waterloo to North Pole in a remarkable 20 minutes. But the nearest it got to polar bears was Acton, where North Pole was their depot, named after a pub. If a railway using a pub name seems unlikely, then remember you can travel on the Tube from Angel to Elephant & Castle on London's Northern line. Or you could try Manor House, Swiss Cottage and Royal Oak. Sadly some pub stations have gone: the capital's Welsh Harp and Kings Arms stations have been closed, the Bricklayers Arms depot has been demolished, and the Jolly Sailor Junction has been renamed the more respectable, but less fun, Norwood Junction. Elsewhere, you can still include in your British railway round these: Craven Arms (Shropshire), Portsmouth Arms (Devon), Bo Peep Junction (Sussex), Berney Arms (near Great Yarmouth) - which station and pub cannot be reached by road but only by train, foot or boat - and the best of the bunch, Bat And Ball station (near Sevenoaks, Kent).

JUST THE TICKET: You might think that 400 New York City subway cars would have to get quite a speed up to end up in the ocean off the Delaware coast. In fact they are obsolete ones and were dropped off ships, intended to serve as artificial reefs. You just hope the fish don't end up like commuters - packed in like, well, sardines. Old military tanks and naval ships are also being sunk there to give a home to wildlife in an otherwise featureless sea bottom.

A STEAM LOCO at the mountain summit of the Settle & Carlisle Railway, England's highest main line, once spun round like one of those wind-driven advertising signs on its turntable and, the story goes, could only be stopped by the fireman shovelling coal onto the circular track the thing rotates on. Clearly it was a problem, because the turntable was afterwards barricaded in with a stockade of sleepers (ties) to keep the wind out.

NOT FAR away on the Furness Railway on the Cumbrian coast a steam locomotive plunged into a hole that opened up into old iron workings on September 22, 1892. The crew jumped clear, and repair men managed to crane the tender out, but if you want an entire vintage steam engine, it's still there, about 200ft down. Over 40 more locos lie in abandoned mines around Britain.

THE trouble with building canals is that water needs to be flat, so has to follow contours or use cuttings, tunnels and aqueducts to deal with hills, or else face complex solutions for raising boats. The canal lock with two gates is familiar but in earlier times primitive canal schemes involved simply deepening a river, such as the Thames at Oxford, by building weirs every few miles and then opening a boat-shaped gate to allow water to pour through and a boat to shoot down with it. There were called 'flash locks' presumably because they were quick. Pulling a boat up this waterfall with ropes and horses must have been harder. Alternatively the level of the whole reach above was lowered by opening the gate, then the boat pulled through, the gate closed - followed by a very, very long wait for the river to refill.

SWINGING TIME: What about a section of canal, 234ft long, and up in the air, that can swing sideways through 90 degrees complete with water, a boat floating on it, and, if you will, a bargee sitting on the roof smoking his pipe? This sounds like an idea that wouldn't hold water, but it can be seen at the Barton Swing Aqueduct at Barton-on-Irwell, west of Manchester.

UPWARDS AND ONWARDS: Swinging a canal sideways is impressive enough, but upwards would be a fine trick. This can be seen at the enormous Anderton Boat Lift, two-and-a-half miles north-west of Northwich, Cheshire. It can lift two canal boats at a time, in a pair of enormous caissons full of water, from the River Weaver up to the Trent and Mersey canal. It looks like it shouldn't work - but it does.

DRAMA: Even more dramatic is the beautiful and unique Falkirk Wheel in Scotland (above) which lifts a section of canal while balancing it with another, in a rotating cylinder shape. And a massive Canadian boat lift at Peterborough, Ontario, requires no power to operate, because the upper chamber fills with more water than the lower one, more than counterbalancing it and lifting 1,300 tons nearly 20 metres. There's another Canadian one at Kirkfield, Ontario.

Railway 'Frog Wars' - see Page 12

9 Ships and navigation: Enough oddities to sink a battleship

THE 17TH CENTURY GPS - A WOUNDED DOG: In the 17th century there was a great need to discover your longitude at sea, for thousands of men were dying in wrecks caused by navigation errors, and, probably more important at the time, valuable cargoes were being lost.

If the correct time at the home port could be known on board ship, then the difference between that time and the time on board (measured by the sun) would tell the longitude (north-south, that is; latitude, east-west, being more easily fixed).

In 1687 the utterly extraordinary Wounded Dog method of finding the time at the home port, and therefore longitude, was proposed. There was a new 'medicine' on sale called Powder of Sympathy which, its followers believed, could not only speed the curing of a wound but do it at any distance. The powder's 'discoverer', Sir Kenelm Digby, claimed to have found that if the bandages of a wounded person, left behind somewhere, were dipped in a solution of these quackish powders, that person would jump at that very moment.

The proposal was for each ship to take a wounded dog aboard and at noon in the home port a servant would dip the bandages in the liquid, causing the dog on board to yelp suddenly. Even if this crackpot scheme worked, wouldn't it have required a dog to be freshly wounded on board regularly? What if it yelped for some other reason near the expected time? It seems inhumane by modern standards, but then up to this point many sailors were blind in one eye as a result of staring at the sun to make navigational measurements. In the end the Wounded Dog Method was not adopted, and it was John Harrison's chronometer that allowed accurate home-port time to be carried on board, as recounted in Dava Sobel's brilliant and most readable book *Longitude*.

SIGNAL BOATS: One of the barmier solutions to the longitude problem was the idea of stationing hundreds of signal boats along trade routes to fire cannon at noon and midnight. How these were to be anchored in water sometimes miles deep, and who would man them despite hurricanes, icebergs, war or pirates was beyond belief, and of course even if a ship heard such a signal, the speed of sound would distort the time, and this speed varies according to atmospheric pressure on that day. Even later, it was suggested attaching something like these 'signal boats' to huge rockets and firing them into the sky, where they would sail along at 12,600 miles high without anchors and they could signal down to ships, the comparisons between three of the signals giving a very precise fix, as a sailor might take a fix from the bearings of three landmarks on a coast. Barmy though it all seems, this is the system we use today. The 'signal boats' are satellites, the signals radio waves not cannon blasts, and the whole unlikely caboodle known as the Global Positioning System, or GPS.

GPS: The time delay of the signal from any of the 30 satellites reaching a GPS receiver gives the distance from that satellite, and as long as three are 'visible', your precise position. The astonishing precision of the system down to a metre or less was initially available only to the military, presumably for targetting (so a cruise missile could hit a car windscreen), the civilian version giving more like a 50-metre fix. The system is provided free by the United States as a worldwide public service, although what evil use the world might put it to is demonstrated by the fact that exported American GPS receivers mysteriously stop working at 1,000 knots speed and at 60,000ft in altitude. Hmmm. Probably not thinking of yacht owners, then!

Meanwhile European pride (for which one can usually read 'French') meant that they had to set about producing a totally unnecessary set of different satellites for their own GPS system. If you think this exaggerates Gallic pride, consider the moment when in 1884 the whole world at a conference decided to use the Greenwich Meridian as the prime meridian for time-keeping, navigation and geography. The French alone persisted in drawing maps with a different one, the Paris Meridian, for another 27 years. And even after that, as author Dava Sobel recalls, they couldn't bring themselves to use the words Greenwich Mean Time, but called it 'Paris Mean Time, retarded by nine minutes twenty-one seconds.' Retarded, *moi*?

BTW, the GPS system is officially called NAVSTAR. That is an acronym standing for, well, nothing at all. It's just that someone at the U.S. Department of Defense thought it sounded cool. And time goes slightly faster in orbit, as Einstein predicted, so the clocks have to be continually corrected.

PORT AND STARBOARD: Spacecrews use terminology from Viking invaders probably called Hagar the Horrible or Olaf the Old or something like that. Boats such as Viking longships had a steering board, a kind of big flat oar, lashed on the right, looking forward, so that side is *starboard,* thought to stand either for steering board or steering side. You'd not want to damage it by tying up on that side, so the other side, that is left looking forwards, was *port*, where the port was. This, and the associated red/green colours apply to aircraft, helicopters, submarines, spacecraft, etc.

'*Larboard'* is an archaic word for port (probably meaning loading side), but obviously when shouted on the wind was too like starboard, so the existing alternative word *port* was enforced (starting with Fitzroy, captain of *HMS Beagle*, Darwin's ship).

That these terms are necessary must become apparent even to landlubbers when you think of a captain standing at the bow (front!) looking back and shouting 'let off the left hand ropes' to crew standing looking forwards. It would be chaos. Or the crew of a spacecraft docking, advising the oncoming one: 'Turn left a little...' Equally disastrous.

IF IT'S hard to remember which goes with which, consider this: *Port, Red, Left, Can* are all shorter words than *Starboard, Green, Right, Cone*. If you are wondering what *can* and *cone* are doing there, they are the shapes of buoys, or the topmarks on posts, heading up river, passed on the relevant side. So you have your *red port* light near the *red* buoy which is *can*-shaped on the *left*. Short and simple. (Except in America, South Korea, Philippines and Japan where buoyage is reversed - because, British sailors joked, you'd be wanting to leave those places, not get there).

TITANIC ERROR? The *Titanic* film starring Kate Winslet was widely criticised for getting this wrong when they spotted the iceberg ahead, on the starboard (right) bow. The officer yells to the helmsman 'Hard a starboard' which seems odd as he needs to turn to port (left) which the ship indeed does (but not far enough, you won't need reminding). Except that it was at this time usual to give helm orders as if the old tillers (as still used on small boats) existed, where you need to pull or push the tiller in the direction you *don't* want the bows to go. So the order *would* have been given like that. The Vikings would have understood.

EAST GOES WEST: Points of the compass can be confusing too. The origin of the word north, the Proto-Indo-European root '*ner-*', meant - rather uselessly - left. This makes sense if you consider that if you look at the sunrise from anywhere, north *is* left. The Latin word *auster* meaning south, as in Australia, actually had its origins in a word meaning east. One suggested explanation for the confusion is that from the Italian peninsula, both directions were towards the same sea.

LOG AND KNOTS: A ship's *log*, meaning the speed measuring device not the confusingly same-named book, was a real log at first, tossed over the bow and timed going past. Later on a rope with a disc on the end was thrown over and the number of knots in the rope that passed out in time measured by a sandglass gave the speed – in *knots*.

SWINGING THE LEAD: The phrase meaning to skive, waste time or do things badly comes from the job of sounding depths, as with a ship or boat feeling its way through uncertain waters. A good sailor would throw the lead weight on its thin rope forward in an Admiralty-approved method of whirling it round in circles and flinging it far ahead, then pulling the rope until it was taut but not

lifting the lead just as it passed vertical. A bad or lazy sailor would merely *swing the lead* underhand, which was supposed to be used only with very slow boats in shallow water.

MARK TWAIN: The various depths in fathoms would be marked by different coloured bands on the rope, and the depths would be called back to the skipper. One such call would be 'Mark Twain', meaning mark of two fathoms. This would be particularly common in a shallow river like the Mississippi, navigated by flatbottomed paddleboats. This is where Samuel Clemens got his pen name, Mark Twain, (although he was inspired to do so by another earlier writer). The sounding lead had a hollow in its base filled with tallow or grease, and when pulled up for the next swing the nature of the bottom – mud, sand, gravel, or clean for rock etc – could be called back to the skipper. 'Mark Twain, sandy bottom!' The sonar of its day.

IT'S A SQUARE MEAL: Sailors in the Royal Navy had square wooden plates with raised edges to avoid spillage in heaving seas. If the dinner reached the corners, it was literally a *square meal*, as we still say.

TWO SHEETS TO THE WIND: Sheets on sailing vessels are not the sails, as landlubbers might reasonably think, but the ropes tied to their corners to control them. In a strong wind, they go dangerously flapping and whipping around if let go and can be hard to get back, while this means the boat is out of control. Hence a sailor who is drunk is said to be two or *three sheets to the wind*.

SHOW A LEG: Women could sometimes go to sea in the old sailing ships, and when the men were roused for their watches were in danger of also being tipped out of hammocks by bosuns for being tardy. So the cry '*show a leg*' applied to females who were often smuggled aboard and would indicate with their relatively petite feet and hairless legs (one supposes) that they were not to be tipped out.

THE DEVIL TO PAY: The top deck of wooden sailing ships was kept watertight against rain and waves by caulking, that is forcing oakum (old rope, unravelled by paupers for a pittance, hence '*money for old rope*') and tar into the long cracks between the deck planks. This was messy and hard work. The worst such joint was 'the devil' between the top of the vessel's sides and the first deck plank, for there was no room to pay out (unwind) the oakum, it was *the devil to pay*. And there was even less space between *the devil and the deep blue sea*.

THE SLUSH FUND: The poor quality meat, such as salted beef or cheap pork, which was boiled up in large tureens by cooks on such ships, caused a fatty scum known as slush to float to the top. This was skimmed off and kept in a barrel. Ashore, the fatty slush was sold to make soap or treat pulleys etc. The resulting *slush fund* was divided up among the crew.

TWO, SIX, HEAVE! is the usual cry when British Boy Scouts or village tug o' war teams etc want to pull something together. Why the funny numbering? It's because in a six-man gun crew, numbers two and six would pull the ropes to replace the gun knocked back by the recoil, and this was the order to ensure they pulled together.

COLD ENOUGH TO FREEZE THE BALLS OFF A BRASS MONKEY: The most frequently quoted origin is that a monkey was a metal frame that held a pyramid of cannon balls close to a naval gun without letting them roll around, and when it was really cold the balls would fall off. A glance at the science shows that difference in the two metals' coefficient of expansion is not different enough to cause this, and you'd be mad to stack cannon balls in a pitching and tossing ship (they were stored flat in a wooden holder). However, there was a cannon called a brass monkey, and cannon have tails, so sailors as usual were looking for something ruder to express how cold it was. It's just said for humorous emphasis. More recently sailors also said: 'It's as cold as a witch's tit in a brass bra' and you don't suppose

they had many of those on board either. Actually with the modern Royal Navy, you never quite know...

CHOC-A-BLOCK was when a rope was being pulled through a pulley block to pull in another pulley block, such as one on the end of a wooden boom, yard, or attached to a load. When the blocks are touching, there's no point in pulling any more. *Choc-a-block* came by extension to mean anything packed tight. The slang for testicles, *bollocks*, also comes from this root.

HERMAPHRODITES AND SPANKERS: Are proper nautical terms. A *hermaphrodite* rig is a non-standard mix of fore-and-aft sails and square sails on a sailing vessel; also known as a jackass rig. A *ship* is a particular rig too, and not any sailing vessel. The sailing boats that take part in the famous Tall Ships Race are nearly always *not* ships. A *spanker* is a fore-and-aft extra sail set on a square-rigged sailing vessel.

BY AND LARGE: Sailing qualities of ships were checked in two main dimensions: By the wind, meaning sail close to it, and sailing large, that is with all possible sails spread widely to catch a following wind. If the ship was satisfactory in both directions, it was reported as good *by and large*.

LOBLOLLY BOYS, POWDER MONKEYS AND DEAD BABIES: From sailing warships. A loblolly boy was a boy, or man, who assisted the surgeon in a blood and gore-covered sick bay, heating irons for searing wounds, applying alcohol to those about to undergo amputation, throwing limbs overboard, and named after the porridge the sick were given. Powder monkeys were the boys, men or at times women whose job it was to pass gunpowder from the magazine up through hatches (in a human chain) and then run the length of the deck to keep guns supplied, as enemy shot was passing through and causing oak splinters to fly like shrapnel - very hazardous. Dead baby was a soupy stew with bundles of suet which would rise to the top, like an infant chucked in a pond.

LOOSE CANNON: One of these wheeled monsters weighing a ton or more could clearly kill people if it came loose on a ship pitching and tossing around, hence the political metaphor for someone causing trouble, better kept in their place, potentially dangerous. (A loose *canon* on the other hand would be a Church of England official with moral problems).

OTHER naval phrases we use every day without thinking, some more obvious than others, include: *Piping hot* **(straight from the galley, announced by the bosun's pipe),** *To clear the decks* **(for action),** *To go by the board* **- to go over the side of a ship (like a falling mast),** *To be carried away* **– mast, sail or yard etc that breaks in a storm,** *To be in the Doldrums, Show someone the ropes, Over a barrel* **(or to** *kiss the gunner's daughter***) - to be tied over & beaten, to have or be given** *plenty of leeway* **(space between you and something downwind),** *To be taken aback* **(a sail that backs and momentarily stops the boat), its close relative** *sailing too close to the wind, To be pooped* **(get a wave over the stern, a shock, a nuisance and possibly dangerous).**

BRITS like to moan about how Hollywood always includes Americans in some triumph that they didn't actually perform – e.g. seizing the Enigma codes in World War II, or conquering Everest. But if they ever make a film about Americans fighting at the Battle of Trafalgar (1805), they'd be dead right. One of the causes of the War of 1812 between America and Britain was the habit of the British of impressing captured American crews by the thousands into the Royal Navy (that's impressing them in the sense of press-gang, not telling them tall stories). But you have to judge it by the standards of the day – the British crews in those days were rounded up by press gangs and thousands of men in the battle (and one or two women) had never been to sea before, which makes their victory over the much larger combined fleets of France and Spain all the more remarkable.

COAL-POWERED SUBMARINES, SUBMARINE AIRCRAFT CARRIERS, SUBMARINES CARRYING A BATTLESHIP-SIZED GUN: All completely and utterly mad, so all built and tried and all sank. (Yes, they are *supposed* to sink, but they didn't come up again). Actually the enormous coal/steam submarine often ran pretty well if you remembered to put the fire out before submerging. A sailing submarine was once tried in America (on the surface, obviously) but this seems to have been a one-off bit of fun with the mast extended through the conning tower.

SUBMARINE THAT ATTACKED A RAILWAY: Subs return home flying Jolly Roger pirate flags they make, showing the ships they have sunk in white outline, or coloured bars. One

British sub in the Second World War returning from a patrol off North Africa showed in outline a railway locomotive and a road truck. It transpired that the boat had surfaced in a bay and shelled and destroyed these with its deck gun. The macabre 'Jolly Roger' flags flown on return to base usually showed white bars for enemy ships sunk, daggers for commando raids, etc. This remarkable one from HMS Ursula shows two trains destroyed, and oil tanks and a factory – all on dry land!

RAILWAYMAN WHO ATTACKED A SUBMARINE: At Liverpool Street station in London may be seen a moving memorial to Captain Charles Fryatt. In 1915 he was master of an unarmed railway ferry running from Harwich to neutral Holland when a German submarine surfaced and ordered him to stop, or be sunk. The captain ordered 'full ahead both' and turned to ram the submarine, which crash-dived to escape. The Imperial German Navy was thus reduced to an international laughing stock, so in 1916 surrounded the ferry with six destroyers, and captured the master, took him ashore in Belgium and shot him by firing squad.

The captain's grave at Dovercourt near Harwich is blunter than the Liverpool St memorial in its inscription: 'Captain Charles Fryatt, Illegally Executed by the Germans.' (Like shooting nurse Edith Cavell in the same conflict, it was another propaganda disaster for the Germans.) Dozens of shells were later fired at the German trenches with the inscription 'To Capt Fryatt's murderers' on them (above).

DEEPLY UNLIKELY: Would be a submarine having a running battle with cavalry, or a submarine attacking a camel train. Ludicrous, even. But both happened in World War I as British submarines penetrated the Dardanelles and attacked Ottoman land targets.

GALE WARNINGS: No one had thought of warning seafarers, and the public in general, of bad weather until Vice Admiral Robert Fitzroy thought it might be sensible after the loss of the ship *Royal Charter* in 1859. Fitzroy (also on Page 111) decided that if there was a Meteorological Office which could co-ordinate weather reports and predict the next few days, lives would be saved. He invented a name for these: 'Weather forecasts', a whole new concept. He had 'Fitzroy storm glasses' (barometers) sent to small fishing villages to warn crews of impending storms.

He devised a system of hoisting cones as gale warnings in ports, ordering fleets not to set sail. The fleet owners were furious at the interruption, and Fitzroy - a somewhat stormy personality himself - eventually lost a fortune trying to serve the public. He cut his own throat in despair, and the system of weather forecasts was abandoned.

But later it was resumed, and has since saved thousands of lives - plus given us today's daily weather forecast in newspapers and TV, shipping forecasts on radio (Blur's Damon Albarn tunes into these). Fitzroy – who was Charles Darwin's captain on The Beagle and gave him a book suggesting landscape could have evolved not been created – had a mountain in Argentina, a place in the Falklands, a tree and a dolphin species, two ships and a sea area for shipping forecasts (appropriately) all named after him in gratitude.

10 Read all about it! Myriad media marvels

FILM TRAILERS in cinemas illogically precede the main film, and don't trail them. In fact to 'trail' something on say, radio, has become a verb for *advance* promotion, equally daft linguistically. But trailers *did* trail films originally. In early cinemas you paid to see a film as many times as you wished (they were shorter than today's, an hour being considered long). As with films on some long-haul planes today, you simply joined in at whatever point the film had reached, saw it to the end, and then watched the beginning if you'd missed it.

The trailer was spliced onto the last reel of the film not only to advertise to the captive audience waiting to see the bit they had missed, but to give those who had watched the film more than once a bit of a shove and get them out of their seats. And come back next week. The very first trailer was in New York, 1912, and followed the end of the first episode of a thriller *The Adventures Of Kathlyn,* where the heroine had been thrown into a lion's den. The trailer said (in writing, of course, silently): 'Does she escape the lion's pit? See next week's thrilling chapter!'

FILM STILLS used in posters and press photos *never* appeared in the films concerned. They needed to be taken on a completely different kind of camera. Movie pictures flicker past at 26 frames a second and use a small area of film, because a degree of blur doesn't matter in movement, whereas a quality still for a poster needed a large format film or plate. So the action was stopped or a session of posing done at the end of the day's shoot. Additionally, there was a long period where films were in colour and newspapers were still in black and white, so 'film stills' supposedly extracted from the film, would have been doubly useless.

THE PARAKEETS which infest South-West London with their

startling green plumage and loud cries all descend from a flock which escaped when *African Queen* was being filmed at nearby Shepperton studios.

WRONG PLACE: Nearly every Hollywood or British film was shot in the wrong place. *Casablanca* was shot in Burbank, California; so was the movie *Morocco* (1930). Morocco itself was used for much of *Lawrence of Arabia* and films set in the Bible lands. Spain stood in for Russia in *Dr Zhivago*. Virtually no Vietnam war films were shot in Vietnam: *The Killing Fields* was shot in Phuket, Thailand, while Stanley Kubrick's *Full Metal Jacket* was filmed in London's Docklands and Bassingbourne, Hertfordshire because Kubrick had developed a morbid fear of flying and couldn't return to Hollywood. Hertfordshire and Ireland also stood in for France in *Saving Private Ryan,* whereas Surrey was the Ardennes for *Band of Brothers*. The Himalayas in *Seven Years In Tibet* were, in fact, the Andes.

WHAT SOUND OF MUSIC? When the all-time hit musical *The Sound of Music* first arrived as a film (above) in Korea, one cinema owner found it too long for his programme so shortened it - by cutting out all the uninteresting (to him) musical scenes, keeping the story line about the escaping nun and family intact.

EXPLOSIVE ACTION MOVIES: Early film stock which was nitrate based turned out to be highly combustible and when stored for a long time would self ignite and even explode in cans. Equally, magnetic video or sound tape deteriorates by printing highlights from one moment to the adjoining layer on the reel (so you get a ghost sound of the one coming up, for example). You have to keep recording old recordings.

BLOODY NEWSPAPERS! The M in red on the spine of your newspaper, probably with three other colours in CKMY, which helps printers line up the bright pink ink with the others, is M only because of a bloody slaughter. A new bright red-blue dye was named after the recent 1859 Battle of Magenta in the war between the Austrian empire and the French second empire/Piedmontese. The source of the dye was a tar sludge made when manufacturing coal gas, used all over Europe. Another dye named after another bloody battle around the same time is Solferino, a purple and also an 1859 battle. Such was the carnage in these two battles – after which the victors went round bayoneting the screaming wounded to death – that this led to the formation of the Red Cross. All this connection between dyeing and dying didn't prevent these colours, and the earlier discovery of mauve, sweeping the world of ladies' fashion for several years.

CYAN: Another letter on the printers' colour register is C and is also connected with death. It stands indirectly for cyanide, the deadly poison. Cyan, a blue-green, when first created reminded people of Prussian Blue, a tint which contained cyanide.

KEY: The last colour registration letter is K for black, the usual colour of death, so called because it is the 'key' colour. Key meaning it is printed first to get the other colours lined up. In fact black can be made by mixing the other three, but it is expensive, likely to go wrong and with fine detail, such as these words, printing could produce blurring. Mixed colours do this when out of register, as printers put it, and the CKMY and other marks on the spine are intended to combat this error. On the other hand newspapers do mix those colours to make large areas of black seem blacker than black, the apparent nonsense of 'four-colour black' being richer and darker than plain black.

Y NOT: So Y is the only one standing for a commonly recognisable colour and nothing deadly: Yellow. It could still be an insult. As in 'Yellow press!'

THE CKMY printing process seems to add colours. It doesn't. It *subtracts* them, leaving the colour you wish to see. Whereas RGB (red, green, blue) colour blending on video screens adds colour. Proof: If you blend all the CKMY colours, you get black. If you blend the RGB colours, you get white.

SILENCE: Millions of pounds have been spent in Britain over the years broadcasting the two minutes' silence on radio on Remembrance Day. Why not use last year's, you may reasonably ask. BTW, automatic equipment which cuts in light music in case of prolonged silence on radio has to be disabled to allow this.

PLUG: The verb to plug a product comes from Captain Leonard Plugge (1889-1991) who started Britain's first pirate radio station, that is the first to carry advertising in spite of the ban on it during radio's first few decades and thus break the BBC's monopoly. The station, Radio Normandy, was hugely successful in the run-up to World War II and recorded shows on 78rpm discs in Britain and sent them to France for transmission back to the UK. Roy Plomley, who later invented the world's longest-running radio programme Desert Island Discs, became a star with Radio Normandy, and the car firm that became Jaguar was launched by its advertising. Capt Plugge started off in the drawing room of a director of Benedictine distillers in Fecamp in 1931 and ended up with a chain of transmitters in France and Ireland, a success only stopped by the War.

SING BING: The great mid-20th century crooners, starting with Bing Crosby, didn't come about by accident. They came about by technological necessity. The radio microphones, gramophones and wireless sets of the time could transmit baritone singing very well, down to a warm intimacy never before achieved, whereas bass and soprano would have to carry on with their controlled yelling suited to huge theatres. Thus the careers of Crosby (below), Sinatra, Bennett and the rest were created by a humbly glowing radio valve.

SPACED OUT: CDs cases are the size they are - just under half the width of the previous 12 inch vinyl LPs - so that record shops could utilise the existing shelves with a spacer for two rows of CDs where one row of LPs sat before.

THERE IS NO reason why DVD boxes need to be bigger

than CD cases, because the discs are the same size. But because they replaced VHS videos, the boxes were made the same height so they could be displayed side-by-side with videos during the changeover. Now we're stuck with it.

WRONG BONG: The bronzed oiled hunk who hit the gong at the start of Rank films, in a theatrical gesture to rival MGM's snarling lion, never hit the thing – because it was made of papier mache. Ken Richmond, who died in 2006 aged 78, always said: 'If you hit that gong, you would have gone straight through.' He was the fourth gonger but the dubbed-in sound was in fact made by James Blade, who earlier made the V-for Victory signal put out by BBC radio to occupied Europe during the war to encourage resistance.

ODDEST BRITISH NEWSPAPER NAMES:
The Royston Crow
The Falmouth Packet
The Banbury Cake

ODDEST AMERICAN NEWSPAPER NAMES:
The Oxford Eccentric
The Acorn, California
The Headlight, New Mexico
The Avalanche-Journal, Texas
The Ripple, North Carolina
The Fresno Bee, California
The Daily Titan, Fullerton, California
The Doings, Illinois

PERSISTENT THEMES IN NEWSPAPER NAMES:

Astronomical – *Sun, Star, Comet, Planet, World, Globe, Universe.*

Transmission method – *Mail, Dispatch, Tablet, Post, Express, Signal, Pantagraph, Telegram, Telegraph, Transcript, Letter, Press.*

Announcements – *Clarion, Bugle, Echo, Bulletin, Voice, Trumpet.*

Symbolic figure - *Standard, Herald, Courier, Citizen, Sentinel, Tribune, Worker, Leader, Guardian, Observer, Eagle.*

Geographical – *Dominion, Nation, Empire.*

Chronological – *Times, Time, Day, Age, Week.*

Achingly dull – *Journal, Advertiser, Diary, Recorder, Register, Chronicle, Review, News.*

YOUR TITLES PRODUCE SHEER HORSEPOO! The Express, the Telegraph, the Economist, the Times, the Independent and The Star were all names of London stage coaches in the early-mid-19th century.

NO NEWS: In the first weeks of radio broadcasting from London, they dropped the news programme one day because, they said, nothing had happened.

LISTENING to your car radio while parked in Parliament Square, London, you will hear the bongs of Big Ben *before* you hear them through the car window. The reason being that radio waves travel at the speed of light, far faster than the speed of sound. But listen to them on digital and it will be the other way round, because of a built-in delay, making precise timings useless.

TWO-WAY TELEVISION: Many people shown television for the first time thought it was a two-way medium. A London schoolgirl who saw a demonstration of the new machine in 1925 recalled: 'We all clapped politely because we were rather frightened of television. I think the trouble was we believed that, if they could make this film, they could see into our houses. We could see them, they could see us.' In 1948 George Orwell brought the nightmare of the all-seeing telescreens to his novel *Nineteen Eighty-Four*.

GREAT WRONG PREDICTIONS *(Nos 7-9)!*
Television won't matter in your lifetime or mine.
Rex Lambert in The Listener, 1936.

The problem with television is that people must sit and keep their eyes glued to the screen; the average American family hasn't time for it... television will never be a serious competitor of broadcasting [by which they meant radio of course].
New York Times editorial, 1933.

Television? The word is half Greek, half Latin. No good can come of it.
C. P. Scott (who may, on reflection, have been *half* right).

TEST CARDS: Until the 1960s, it was illegal for British children's programmes to run into adult ones in case they kept watching. The Test Card, a pattern of lines used for tuning new televisions, had to be shown for at least 10 minutes to get the critters to clear off. The programme *Tonight* broke the ban. If you are too young to recall them, one is pictured above. The X on the child's blackboard had to be the centre of the screen. An eccentric British society, the Test Card Circle, meets in order to watch these designs and the rather strange music that used to be broadcast with them.

FREELANCE, as in journalist, originally meant a knight whose lance was for hire.

CURIOUS ORIGINAL BOOK/FILM TITLES:
George Orwell's *Nineteen Eighty-Four* was planned to be called *The Last Man in Europe*. It was intended to come out in 1948, so he reversed the date. His real name, BTW, was Eric Blair.
Joseph Heller's *Catch 22* was going to be called *Catch 18* but just before it was published someone used the number 18 in a title, so it was changed at random.
Pride and Prejudice – First Impressions.
Gone with the Wind - Mules in Horse Harness.
Coronation Street – Florizel Street.
Sherlock Holmes (the character) – Sherrinford Holmes.

LARGEST BOOK yet published was *Bhutan: A Visual Odyssey Across the Kingdom* by Michael Hawley, a scientist at the Massachusetts Institute of Technology. It is 5ft by 7ft, has 112 pages and weighs 133lb. Published in 2003, it cost

$10,000 a copy but for that you got a free easel to stand it on. This included $8,000 for an educational charity, Friendly Planet, operating in that part of the world.

THIS was outdone in terms of shelf width, weight and cost by the *Oxford Dictionary of National Biography*, published the following year, 2004. This contained 60 million words in 54,922 essays in 60 volumes, weighed 280lb and took up 11ft of very strong shelf space. Only around £7,500 per copy.

DIGITAL RADIO was pushed as better sound than FM (VHF) which is replaced. In fact, in Britain at any rate, it's worse, because it is so compressed that much of the information is left out. Some of the music isn't even stereo, which FM was. Because of time delays, the Big Ben bongs (above) are wrong on digital, as are the time pips.

EQUALLY CDs were pushed as better than vinyl LPs, but on a blind listening, switching from one to the other, most people found they weren't. They were more profitable, more convenient, more copiable, more compact and more durable.

THAT last claim about modern digital media being more durable isn't *always* true. Libraries have 11th century parchments and embroideries recording various things, and Egyptian hieroglyphics recording tax affairs go back millennia. Yet digital recordings from the 1960s and 1970s in various formats – 12inch video discs (above), large floppy

disks, certain tape systems – are utterly unplayable because the software or hardware doesn't exist any more, or because the material has deteriorated.

A COMPUTER virus is supposed to do things like slow your computer down significantly, be almost impossible to get rid of, annoy you with unwanted messages on the screen day and night and aggressively demand money from you with the threat of worse malfunctions, perhaps going on for years. Yet all this is exactly what at least one well known computer virus protection software does to unwitting purchasers.

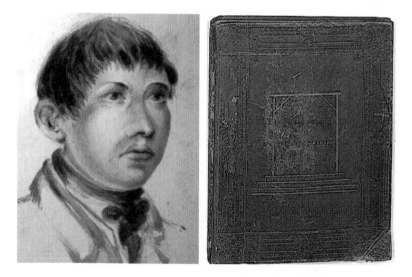

ANTHROPODERMIC bibliopegy means covering books in human skin – not something you may wish to browse through for a relaxing read! There is one such book (above right) in the Bristol Record Office. It was made from the skin of John Horwood (above left) hanged at Bristol's new prison in 1821 after murdering Eliza Balsum, with whom he was obsessed. The book, giving the full details of the murder, shows a gallows on the cover. Horwood's skeleton was kept in a cupboard at Bristol University, with the noose still around its neck, for exactly 190 years to the hour from his execution – it was then, in 2011, buried at last. Five books in

USA college libraries are confirmed to have this deeply gruesome covering. Mostly from executed murderers.

APPROPRIATELY BLURB: American humorist Frank Gelett Burgess (1866-1951) invented a character Miss Belinda Blurb and first used the term for the stuff inside a book cover. Blurb became a verb eventually.

PUBLISHERS have a habit of rejecting books (including this one, the fools!). But then J. K. Rowling's first Harry Potter book was rejected, no fewer than 12 times, and it was only accepted after one publisher's nine-year-old daughter insisted on knowing how the book ended. Result: tens of millions of books sold in every part of the world. Gone With The Wind by Margaret Mitchell was rejected an appalling 38 times, yet became America's best seller. T.S Eliot, the poet, was the director at Faber & Faber who turned down George Orwell's Animal Farm, declaring it 'unconvincing', BTW, Eliot was also the primary school teacher of a very different poet, John Betjeman, who gave him a book of poems, aged 9.

FRUIT OF THE WEB: The entire contents of the internet weighs as much as two strawberries.

11 Place names and geography: The insane places we live in

PLACE NAMES in the United States reflect the fact that this huge land was settled very quickly by immigrants who quickly used up all the names familiar from their home countries. So we end up with names about features in that spot – like Beaver Creek, Bald Knob, Moose Jaw Lake or Boulder – or whimsical, crazy or folksy names for towns and villages. These include:

Azusa, CA, near Los Angeles - One local claims the name came about because the local store sold everything 'from A to Z in the USA'.

Bat Cave, NC – First mammals came by air.

Bugtussle, TN – Backswoods self-mockery.

Cando, ND – Some kind of argument about authority for naming this place led to a local saying: 'We'll show you what we can do, and call it Cando.'

Climax, NY – An odd theme going here. Nearby settlements called Result and Surprise.

Due West, SC – Is actually due east of the original trading post.

Eclectic, AL – Taking the mickey out of an educated resident who said he'd studied an 'eclectic' course of study at school.

Gobblers Knob – There are a staggering 25 places with this unlikely name in the USA.

Frankenstein, MO – No monsters. Gottfried Franken gave land to build a church here in 1890. Near Schubert.

Hell, MI – Possible place of pilgrimage for Norwegians from Hell Junction. A top postmark for people paying, or not paying, divorced spouses.

Kill Devil Hills, NC - According to legend, named after a rum so powerful it would kill the Devil.

Knockemstiff, OH – Again, named after killer local moonshine (illegal liquor).

Lightsville, OH – Is neatly in Darke county, where William B. Light neatly laid out the town.

Notus, ID – A wagon train of settlers stopped here, the story goes. One group, asked if they were ready to continue to Oregon, replied: 'Not us'.

Tick Bite, NC – Not too inviting, frankly.

Truth or Consequences, NM – What a great name. Formerly called Hot Springs; renamed after the radio and TV game show. *That's* a fan base! Near the town of Elephant Butte (hill).

Why, AZ - Named for a Y-shaped intersection of state Highways 85 and 86.

Whynot, NC – They got too fed up with the argument over what to name the place. 'Why not this?' and 'Why not that?' There's another in Mississippi, but why not?

NASTY, UGLEY VILLAGES: Villagers of tiny **Bedlam**, in England's North Yorkshire, are not exactly delighted with the name signs that have been erected there, causing one wag to add 'Twinned with L'Unacy'. No doubt they fear too many sightseers will cause, well, Bedlam. But the novelty will wear off. Inhabitants of **Nasty** and **Ugley**, near-neighbouring villages across the Herts-Essex border, have long since got over jokes about the Nasty Boys Choir or the Ugley Women's Institute. And if people can live in **Pratts Bottom**, Kent, or take jokes about what goes on at **Cuckold's Cross**, Herts, **Over Wallop**, Hants, **Nookie**, Wilts, **Crackpot**, Yorks or **Hell Corner**, Berks then mere Bedlam can take it on the chin. In fact, as with the Bedlam mental asylum once sited where the Imperial War Museum now is, Bedlam village's name probably comes from Bethlehem. Like the modern version of the hospital, they could always compromise with Bethlem.

GEOGRAPHICAL CONFUSION: In Britain is more common than in Paris, Texas with five **Californias**, near Falkirk in Scotland, or Derbys, or Norfolk or Suffolk or Baldock in Herts; three **Gibraltars**, near Bedford, part of Mablethorpe, Lincs, or near Woodbridge, Suffolk; two **New Yorks** in Lincs and Tyne and Wear; a **Moscow**, Ayrshire, a **New Zealand** in Derbys, a **Quebec**, Durham, a **Rhodesia**, Notts and a **Palestine**, nr Andover, Hants (in the latter one travels down Mount Carmel to Zion). The former Australian penal colony of **Botany Bay** seems oddly popular with at least three villages, in Somerset, Kent, and Middlesex, plus countless farms and a Dorset pub named after it. **Little France** in Lothian; **Egypt** in Berkshire; **Normandy** in Surrey, **America** in Cambridgeshire . . . the list of places that aren't what they say is almost endless. If you find these puzzling, there's **Conundrum** in Lothian.

SEASONAL OFFERINGS: In terms of British place names, may be found at **Good Easter** in Essex; **Easter Bush** in Lothian; **Cold Christmas** in Essex; **Christmas Common** in Oxon; and **Christmaspie** in Surrey. The only place with punctuation is **Westward Ho!** in Devon, and the only one, well, of its kind, is **Rest And Be Thankful**, near Arrochar and Inveraray in Argyll.

WEST COUNTRY PLACES: Have a pleasing insanity which even P.G. Wodehouse couldn't have made up. Why is **Toller Fratrum** next to **Toller Porcorum** in Dorset? What goes on at nearby **Ryme Intrinsica**? Or at **Ab Lench** in Worcs, **Praze-an-Beeble** in Cornwall or **Zeal Monarchorum** in Devon?

WELSH GO ON A RARE BIT: The Welsh have a happy habit of running words together in a way that even the Germans might find strange. Taken to an extreme this gives Britain's longest railway station name sign at **Llanfairpwllgwyngyll-gogerychwyrndrobwllllantysiliogogogoch** on the line to Holyhead. Often shortened to Llanfair PG. But it has a real meaning: St Mary's church in the hollow of the white hazel near a rapid whirlpool and the church of St Tysilio near the red cave. Welsh readers would already know that. Also Welsh, **Bwlch**, Powys, the only village without a vowel. In English at any rate.

COMMON AS MUCK: Other British places are staggeringly unusual because of their sheer commonness, if that makes any sense. If you include double-barrelled names or those prefixed or suffixed by South or Common or whatever, **Newtown** has 75, **Middleton**, 35, **Milton**, 46; **Norton**, 40; **Upton**, 33; **Broughton**, 23; **Sutton**, 52; **Weston**, 41; and **Preston**, 28. But in fact there's only one **Muck**, an island in the Inner Hebrides.

ATTACK OF THE GIGGLESWICK: If you like schoolboyish giggling at silly names – and even if you are above all that, you are now going to read this paragraph to see, aren't you? – there's **Feltwell**, Norfolk, **Sandy Balls**, Hants, **Scratchy Bottom**,

Dorset, **Crapstone**, Devon, **Three Cocks**, Powys, **Twatt**, Orkney, and when it comes to roads, **Booty Lane**, Heck, **Sluts Hole Lane**, Cambs, **The Knob**, Kings Sutton, **Back Passage**, EC1, **Bladda**, Paisley, **Hooker Road**, Norwich, **Slag Lane**, Haydock, **Spanker Lane**, Nether Heage, **Juggs Close**, Lewes, **Fanny Hands Lane,** Ludford Parva, **Basque Court, Garter Way,** London SE16. Not remotely funny, of course, no, no, no … and well done locals for not changing it to something bladder – sorry, blander! Still, bet you're glad you don't have to put any of these on your headed notepaper. **Giggleswick** is in N. Yorks.

NOT REALLY THERE: British places that shouldn't really be there at all include **Nowhere** in Kent; five **Nomanslands** in Cornwall, Devon, Hants, Herts and Wilts; **Noplace** in County Durham, two **No Man's Heaths** in Cheshire and Warks; an **Innominate Tarn**, Cumbria; and **Inaccessible Pinnacle** in Skye. **Nonsuch** in Ewell, Surrey really *isn't* there; it was the site of the great Tudor Palace which is gone. But there's still Nonsuch Park.

Jeepers geography

ALL THE CONTINENTS end with the same letter they start with. The rocks at the top of Everest were once in deep sea.

WORLD'S SHORTEST STREET is at Wick in the Scottish Highlands. Ebenezer Place is 2 yd and 9in long and has just one front door in it - No 1 (and only) Ebenezer Place.

NARROWEST STREET is also in Britain, Parliament Street in Exeter, which seems more like a brick alleyway. It is 25in (0.64m) wide, as it were, at its narrowest.

DISCOVERING AMERICA: One fact was largely overlooked in all the 1992 razzmatazz over the 500th anniversary of the discovery of America - as generations of schoolchildren have been taught - by Spaniard Christopher Columbus in 1492. Not just the small detail that he was Italian, rather than Spanish. Nor that he was called Cristoforo Columbo or Cristobal Colon but not Columbus. Nor that he didn't get there first by several centuries - the earlier arrival of Vikings is widely accepted. Let alone the people who already lived there. Nor even that he did not set foot on the American mainland at all in 1492, but on what is now the Bahamas, reaching the mainland in 1495. And even then, he thought he was somewhere near Japan on his way to India. Hence the locals in America being called Indians. It's simply that the very word 'America' originates from the name of a different, almost forgotten Italian explorer, Amerigo Vespucci, who sailed the same seas in the 1490s and published an account of his voyage in 1507. Columbus went down in history, mostly wrongly. But Vespucci had a New World named after him.

WRONG NAMES: Tautological names are those which are grammatical nonsense, **River Avon** (meaning river river) being the most common example in Britain (see below). But even more bonkers is the **Rio Gaudix** in Spain, which means river river river (*Guad* or *Wadi* in Arabic, *Rio* in Spanish, *dix* in Phoenecian). **Bredon Hill** in England means Hill Hill Hill (Brythonic/Old English/Modern English) and king of the lot, **Torpenhow Hill**, England means Hill Hill Hill Hill (Old English *Tor*/Celtic *pen* = head/Anglo-Saxon *how* or *hoe* = spur of high ground/English *hill*). These names come about because successive civilisations wash over constant geographical features, and take the previous name, and add their own word for whatever it is.

EVEN MORE WRONG: Over in Los Angeles we can visit the fascinating **The La Brea Tar Pits**, meaning The The Tar Tar Pits - (Spanish/English) and then there's the **Sahara desert**, meaning Desert desert (Arabic/English). In watery tautology, there's **Eas Fors Waterfall** on the Isle of Mull in Scotland (waterfall waterfall waterfall), **Dal Lake**, Kashmir - (Lake Lake-Balti/English) and in Cornwall the **Hayle Estuary** (Estuary Estuary) near St Ives. It seems to happen anywhere two cultures come into contact. In New Zealand, for example, **Mount Maunganui** means Mount Mount Big (English/Maori).

MAP CHAPS: One of the most civilised things about Britain, Ordnance Survey maps were, in fact, made for crushing truculent Scots. After dealing severely with the Scottish

Jacobite Rebellion in 1746, the Duke of Cumberland said it would have been a lot easier with a proper map of the Highlands. A young Scottish surveyor - most Scots were *against* Bonnie Prince Charlie, not for him, one must recall - called William Roy set off with a surveyor's chain (as in the length, a chain) and a compass. It took nine years. It wasn't for many decades that the rest of Britain was properly mapped by Ordnance (the word after all means weaponry) Survey, so perhaps people in Surrey would have had decent maps far earlier if they had been a lot more rebellious. BTW, each OS map contains deliberate errors, such as kinks in waterways, to catch out illegal copiers. It works.

ENGLISH RIVERS called **Avon** are all a mistake. The Welsh for river is Afon. Clearly they were calling it a river when the English arrived and pushed the Ancient Brits westwards (to become Welsh), presumably stopping to ask politely (they were English, after all) what the waterway was called (before any massacring, raping, pillaging, or whatever went on). That's why there are four Avons in England, at Stratford, Salisbury, Bigbury and Bath. Plus three in Scotland. Plus two in Canada, one in NZ, four in Australia and hundreds in Wales. Even worse tautology is

River Avon Water, a name used in Scotland, meaning River River River.

SCLEROSIS OF THE RIVER: The Brits are staggeringly unoriginal when it comes to river names. There are five **Fromes** in the West Country alone. Two **Rothers** in Sussex. There are several **Brans**, several **Yeos** (two of them nearly touch each other in Devon but don't quite) and many **Stours**.

RHODE ISLAND is by far the smallest U.S. state and also the one with the longest name, being officially 'Rhode Island and Providence Plantations'. It is wrong too; it is not an island and not a plantation.

CANADA is a mistake – the name means village in Iroquoian. When asked what this was called by an explorer in 1534, the locals said this is our village. What? VILLAGE, you thick git!

PEERING AT URANUS: When Astronomer Royal William Herschel discovered what we now call the planet Uranus in 1781 he wanted to call it King George's Star after the monarch. Perhaps they should have stuck with that…

SILLY-BILLY: The French village of Silly near Tours is not that far from Billy, near Blois. When they both had railways stations, a Silly-Billy ticket was possible. But then a Ham-Sandwich journey in Britain was also possible.

12 Mail: The man who posted himself

PILLAR BOXES: British postmen originally wore red (hence round robins and robins on Christmas cards) as in the military uniforms of the day. Pillar boxes are indeed that scarlet red colour today, but oddly *they* were originally green. Air mail postboxes – the service was so new and exciting in the 1920s that it had its own separate boxes - were light blue, like the envelopes today, and the special vans were light blue too. There still is a light blue box in Windsor, Berks.

THE PILLAR BOX was invented by novelist Anthony Trollope. They are now viewed as a British icon, and can be seen around the former Empire, a literally cast iron assurance that your post was safe, the mouth that took all the milestones of your life - before emails were invented.

EXPRESS DELIVERY: Perhaps the most romantic form of post that people have heard of is the Pony Express, an icon of Wild West adventure and endurance which has inspired people ever since. In 1860 it started running between St. Joseph, Missouri to Sacramento, California. The 1,800-mile run took 10 days – and only once was the mail lost. But before that, mail went by ship to Panama, across the isthmus by rail, and back up by ship to California, taking four weeks.

QUICK END: Because the transcontinental telegraph was completed in 1861, the Pony Express didn't last long. And in 1869 the golden spike (the last one fixing the rails down) was driven to join the first transcontinental railroad at Promontory Hill, making the ten-day horse ride seem something out of history, which it soon was. In fact, although it had operated privately to start with, the Pony Express had been an official service for less than four months.

ODDEST NOTICE: Perhaps the oddest notice on a British pillar box was that recalled by politician Tony Benn. The island of Osea, in Essex, where he spent some of his early childhood, was connected to the mainland by a simple causeway which would appear when the tide was low. The postman would cycle across to deliver and collect from the postbox, which bore the probably unique inscription: 'Letters collected according to the tide'.

PIGEON EXPRESS: In February 1897 the world's oddest air mail service started up in New Zealand. Fricker's Great Barrier Pigeongram Agency started providing a faster service for the Great Barrier Island mining community off the Hauraki Gulf to communicate with the nearby city of Auckland. Special lightweight forms similar to today's aerogrammes were used to avoid tiring the birds. Parcels were not accepted. The service lasted until a telegraph cable was laid to the mainland in 1908.

PNEUMATIC POST: People over a certain age will remember pneumatic message systems which ran around department stores, offices, banks etc, with tubes about four inches in diameter delivering messages, cheques, money, medicines etc to remote locations by vacuum suction of capsules shaped like long tin cans. They would whizz along at perhaps 30ft per second and clunk into the receiving bin, the exhauster pump being switched on from the sending end. You needed one tube for each destination, and one return tube for each, so corridors in institutions were festooned with the things, which needed to make sweeping curves. All large newspapers had them for sending copy and photographs to other departments.

PARIS BY TUBE: Although a British invention, the French took pneumatic post (last item) to heart and had La Poste Pneumatique linking all the major post offices in Paris and nearby. The 467-kilometre system was scrapped in 1984, when it was felt that fax (and later email) would replace the demand. In Italy special stamps were issued for Posta Pneumatica, and in Prague a 60km system still exists. Today supermarkets use the system to get money and cheques safely and discreetly from checkout to armoured safes. This, too, may be superseded - by cashless transactions.

IS DELIVERING LETTERS ROCKET SCIENCE? Scotland's short-lived 'Western Isles Rocket Post' in the Hebrides was remarkable for one thing: spectacular failure. On a sunny July Saturday in 1934 German rocket scientist Gerhard Zucher prepared his big moment on the Outer Hebridean island of Scarp and aimed his experimental 4ft aluminium mail rocket across the sound to the bigger island of Harris. He was watched by an MP, two Post Office officials, Government expert Sir Philip Sassoon, and a Press contingent, plus a crowd of locals. He had sealed in the missile 1,200 letters, some addressed to the King and postmarked 'Western Isles Rocket Post'. He pressed the button and there was a loud bang. Charred envelopes fluttered down on spectators from the sky, the rocket being a mangled wreck. Three days later the singed Zucher tried again, in the opposite direction. That failed too.

He blamed the German government for not letting him use the best rocket fuel, and it is true that a few years later Hitler was sending technically better, but considerably less friendly, rockets to the King. The rocket post idea came about because a Scarp islander gave birth to a daughter and needed to deliver her twin. She could not and bad weather prevented her travelling to Harris hospital or calling for help. Eventually she made a perilous boat crossing and the other daughter was safely delivered. There was outrage in Fleet Street that a mighty empire that stretched around the world could ignore a woman in need on the doorstep of Britain. Hence the rocket idea for faster weather-proof messages.

MAIL RAIL: Wouldn't it be great for London if there was some way of getting those red Post Office vans off the congested streets and whizzing letters around unseen, underground? There is – the Post Office's own Underground rail system. But it was closed down to save money in 2003 and waits there disused. Until that date, fifty trains ran 19 hours a day along 23 complicated miles of track, yet no member of the public ever travelled on them, heard them or saw them.

This was Mail Rail, the Post Office's own 2ft gauge system of driverless trains, opened in 1927, for more than 70 years carrying four million letters a day that would otherwise have been in little red vans snarled up by London's traffic. One end is at Paddington, and the other at Whitechapel, and it is still there. It mostly runs at 70ft (21 metres) underground, although it ducks and soars from time to time to pass normal Tube lines and other underground features, such as North London's seven lost rivers.

There are a couple of battery locomotives in siding tunnels for emergency and repair staff to use, so in truth a very few people *have* actually travelled through this unique

system, and one lady who braved the darkness from one end to the other said how very bumpy it was. But there are now moves to give the public rides on the tracks (pictured).

TOUGH JOB being a postman in Vernal, Utah in 1916. The bank there was built with bricks sent from Salt Lake City, all wrapped, labelled and delivered by parcel post because it was half the price of other forms of carriage. Thousands of bricks later, exhausted postmen had the regulations changed. The Bank of Vernal is still known locally as the Parcel Post Bank.

HUMAN POST: Edwardian resident of Forest Hill, South-East London W. Reginald Bray was determined to test the postal service to the limits. He did this by attaching address labels to the strangest things and sending them through the post. Unwrapped. Some, like an old slipper, an onion, a bicycle pump or a half-smoked cigar, were small enough to be pushed into the pillar box. Others, including a bowler hat, a rabbit's skull and a frying pan, had to be taken to the local post office. Eventually, having studied the regulations of the carriage of live animals, he posted himself in 1903 – at the local post office, with a large label attached. The GPO charged the usual 3d per mile plus 1d per pound, up to a shilling. He was delivered by a messenger boy, cycling ahead of him on his own bike, although clearly he knew the way. The 300 yard journey took six minutes. On the doorstep his long-suffering father waited to sign for 'one Inland Registered Person Cyclist', as the docket said.

13 Medical: Do you want to know this?

CONSTIPATION CURE: William Butler did for constipation what Vlad the Impaler did for human rights, and is rightly remembered in a London pub name. A medical quack and physician to James I in the early 17th century, his legacy was for years known widely as *Dr Butler's Purging Ale.* This evil concoction was made by hanging a thin cloth bag containing senna, polypody of oak, very strong spices, agrimony, maidenhair and scurvy grass in a barrel of strong ale. It had a violently laxative effect likened by its victims to the largest cannon used in the Navy. It was sold at pubs or shops with the sign, 'Butler's Head'. One survives in Mason's Avenue, in the City of London EC2, now known as Old Doctor Butler's Head in memory of a man his victims probably would rather have forgotten. Dr Butler probably wouldn't have come to much had he not been approached by King James, who was suffering from an agonising bad back his doctors could not cure. Butler prescribed a barrel of his purging ale – as he did for most patients – and whatever happened next to the king, he forgot about his back. In gratitude he conferred a degree upon Butler and appointed him Court Physician, which went down with the other doctors like a dose of something very unpleasant.

DR BUTLER'S eccentric treatments were deeply unorthodox. For the relief of epilepsy, he would ask a patient to sit still and close his eyes, then fire a pair of pistols either side of his head, inches from his ears. For malaria or the ague, then common, he would throw patients into the Thames head first. For opium overdose, he had a man inserted in the belly of a freshly killed cow. People loved it, and the rich queued up to be maltreated, as some of them still do.

HIRUDOTHERAPY: Is the scientific name for the use of

leeches for medicinal purposes. That is, blood-letting. Oddly, for at least one condition – haemochromatosis, an excessive build-up of iron – that was the right treatment.

FLEAM FLAM: The instrument used for blood-letting was called a fleam.

DISEASE NAMES: Celebrate our former ignorance about their causes. Influenza meant under the influence of stars; malaria meant mal aire - bad air - which was thought to cause it.

ATOM BOMBS led to anaesthesia as well as pain. The development of the atomic bomb in the Manhattan project needed the chemistry for fluorination to be perfected; this led to the creation of modern anaesthetics.

REDHEADS need more anaesthetic than other people.

VISITING doctors working in Yorkshire were given a guide for colloquial ways of discussing health by Doncaster West Primary Care Trust. Terms included:
- **Champion -** *feeling well.*
- **Jiggered -** *feeling unwell.*
- **Right jiggered –** *very unwell.*
- **In the dumps -** *depressed.*
- **Popped his clogs -** *dead.*
- **Gripes -** *abdominal pain.*
- **Gipping -** *vomiting.*
- **Squits, the runs -** *diarrhoea.*
- **Barnsley's playing at home –** *menstruating (that team wear red).*
- **Clock, fizog -** *face.*
- **Noggin -** *head.*
- **Lugholes, tabs -** *ears.*
- **Sneck, snoz -** *nose.*

ASPIRIN was a trademark of the German Bayer company until it was forced to give it up as part of the reparations for World War

I, thus making the drugs available cheaply worldwide. Oddly Heroin was a trademarked Bayer product until 1919 too; the opium-derived product was sold as a cough medicine for children. Yes, for children!

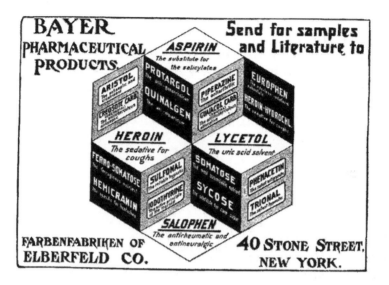

WOBBLY BITS: When English-born American chemist Dr Robert Cheseborough visited oil rigs in Pennsylvania in 1859, he noticed one of the workers cured a burn by applying a sticky petroleum by-product that had gathered around a drill. He researched ways of refining the substance and after more than ten years, called it Vaseline, after the German for water and the Greek for oil. Stores weren't interested in the unattractive product so he loaded a wagon with the stuff and rode across the states, demonstrating it by deliberately burning his arm and then applying the petroleum jelly. Now 15 million jars a year are sold, and a ton of the sticky stuff has been used to protect London marathon runners' wobbly bits from chafing.

ASBESTOSIS was a lung disease that took the world by surprise, after it was realised that thousands of workers who had used the material in roofing, car brakes, pipes or watertanks, fireproofing and insulation material were dying young. This surprise illness and the massive compensation claims that followed in the late 20th century nearly caused the collapse of Lloyd's of London, the global insurance market, and ruined many of the 'names' or investors. But it shouldn't have been so surprising. In AD70 Pliny the Elder noted that slaves weaving asbestos quickly developed a terrible 'sickness of the lungs'. Romans used to throw their asbestos table napkins into the fire to clean them, for the food would burn away, leaving the material unharmed.

COMET VOMIT: In a bizarre forerunner of the great millennium bug scare of the year 2000, as 1910 approached people were terrified that as the Earth passed through the tail of Halley's Comet they would be affected by 'Comet Gas' and this would induce nausea and even death. Credulous people were sold 'Comet pills' by quacks and hucksters against the dire effects of 'Comet gas'. Nothing happened, just as in 2000.

THE industry that grew up in recent decades to remove asbestos safely subsequently charged people billions of pounds for removing material that was often harmless, (although some operators were blameless). On the other hand some types of asbestos *were* certainly lethal – children died who had just sat on the knee of a worker returning home wearing contaminated overalls. At the Swindon works of the Great Western Railway in Britain it was called 'Swindon snow' because it blew around so freely. The apprentices used it to make asbestos 'snowballs' to throw at each other. They died. And so, sadly, did their children.

LESS official doctors' notes were the pencilled codes used on patients' notes to warn of awkward customers, exposed by Bristol University lecturer, broadcaster and GP Phil Hammond in 1997. They were:

- **TATT - tired all the time.**
- **OAP - over-anxious parent.**
- **TEETH - a hypochondriac for whom nothing works -** *tried everything else, try homeopathy!*
- **PAFO relates to someone in casualty who was admitted** *'pissed and fell over'*. **(In British English, pissed means drunk, not angry.)**
- **SIG - stroppy ignorant git.**
- **NFB in Taunton can refer to mentally retarded or slow patients, known colloquially as** *normal for Bridgwater*, **just as NFA in Winchester stands for** *normal for Andover*, **NFN in Norwich means** *normal for Norfolk.*
- **Young male doctors may also boast to their colleagues about how many TUBEs they have performed on female patients. This is not a difficult throat procedure but a** *totally unnecessary breast examination.*
- **More worrying is if your notes are signed TF BUNDY. It means for** *Totally ****** But Unfortunately Not Dead Yet.*
- **Other comments (not Dr Hammond) in the health service include: 'Portsmouth positive'. A senior doctor explained: 'It means they have twice as many tattoos as teeth.'**
- **Notes being computerised means that such quaint practices have become less likely.**

NOT IN VEIN: The heroic doctor who invented the technique of passing a catheter up a vein into the heart did it first by tricking a nurse and getting sacked. In 1929, 25-year-old German doctor Werner Forssmann was forbidden by his professor to try anything so dangerous, or to access the sterile instruments needed. He persuaded a nurse to get them and said he wanted to operate on her to make his breakthrough. She agreed, got on the operating table, and once she was strapped down and couldn't stop him, he operated on himself, passing the catheter into a vein in his arm. He then walked down stairs to the X-ray department to make sure he had reached his heart. This led to his being fired. And to thousands of lives being saved by balloon angioplasty – that is widening blocked arteries by inflating an object inside them. And to a Nobel prize.

FLOSSING your teeth can prevent heart attack. No one knows why.

WOUNDED MASTERS: The world's great Old Masters are created with oil paint. Yet not only was this originally colourless, it was first intended for dressing wounds. Then it was used for protecting paintings made with ordinary paints before it was realised in the early 15th century that colour could be added.

CIGARETTES were prescribed for non-smokers to steady their nerves, particularly for soldiers during and after World War I, and handed out by nurses in hospitals. They were also advertised in that era as good for your throat. The soldiers often eventually died of lung cancer.

WHAT'S more dangerous in terms of human fatalities? Air crashes or donkeys; sharks or coconuts; train crashes or getting out of bed? The latter in all cases. The train figures refers to British passengers and wakers, at the time of writing.

BEING killed by lightning is less likely than being hit by an asteroid. This is a statistical quirk based on the 'fact' that while a few people are killed by lightning every year, when a major asteroid strikes it will probably wipe out many millions, so the risk is higher per person per year.

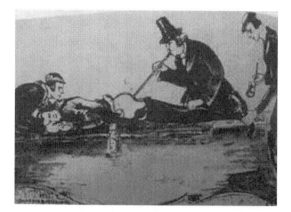

A TOBACCO RESUSCITATION DEVICE invented in Britain in 1774 was supposed to revive victims of drowning by injecting smoke into their bottoms (above). This stimulus of nicotine and warmth was thought to be capable of bringing the apparently dead back to life. The Royal Humane Society placed kits (below), containing tubes and bellows, in wooden boxes along the banks of the Thames, although no one had yet thought of putting more useful life belts and ropes there. There is no record of whether the kits were ever used successfully. Passing tramps may have stolen the tobacco. Certainly if you were half drowned, having some incompetent stranger with a weird device apparently trying to set fire to your rectum may indeed have awoken you.

THE symbol of medicine, Caduceus. Have you ever seen that rather quaint symbol on an American ambulance, the winged staff with two snakes twined round it? A reassuring emblem of old-fashioned selfless doctoring? No, it's the symbol for profit, deceit and greed – it's the *wrong* symbol (above)! It's the staff of Mercury, Roman god of liars and thieves. The one for medicine has one snake and no wings - the rod of Asclepius, symbol of healing (below). So if you're not too ill, check out the symbol when they collect you. We are not going to give in to the temptation to say American medics have got the right one. That would be totally, totally unfair. Sometimes.

14 The human body, sex and all that...

TONGUE: Like fingerprints, everyone's tongue print is different, but taking them at airports might be difficult. The strongest muscle in the body is the tongue.

SNEEZE: If you sneeze too hard, you can fracture a rib. But if you try to suppress a sneeze, you can rupture a blood vessel in your head or neck and die. Tough.

SNEEZY DOES IT: When you sneeze, your heart stops for a millisecond. Hope it starts again. Bless you indeed.

SPEEDY: A powerful sneeze can eject 40,000 droplets at 100mph, so yes they do spread infection. The sneezes caused in some people by bright lights are thought to be a 'faulty wiring' problem. Like the brake lights coming on in a car when you switch the indicators on. Useless.

SIDEBURNS come from the surname of General Burnside (above) in the American Civil War who had large ones. Initially they were 'burnsides' but became sideburns because this sounds better.

FACIAL HAIR: Royal Navy sailors can have a full beard but no moustache on its own, and Royal Marines, who also serve on ships, can have moustaches but no beards. It's Queen Victoria's fault. She thought beards suited only sailors.

CAPITAL IDEA: When you are given a lethal injection in U.S. executions, your skin is swabbed with antiseptic against infection. Equally British hangmen would sew soft leather on the noose to prevent the rope burning the neck, although you might not have had much time to appreciate that kindness.

WOULDN'T BE SEEN DEAD SMILING? A French experimenter made dead people's faces smile, and then look sad, then smile again by controlling the muscles with electrical impulses. These macabre demonstrations were performed by Dr Guillaume-Benjamin-Amand Duchenne (1806-75), who photographed the results, to prove that electrical impulses in the nerves control muscles. Paris Hilton's acting isn't, in fact, controlled this way.

NOT only do some people grow a third set of teeth, which is very rare, but it seems to run in families. On one Las Vegas man who had done so, an X-ray showed a *fourth set* developing underneath. At the American average of $2 per tooth left by the tooth fairy, this could prove expensive for parents.

THERE are only five tastes: sweet, sour, salt, bitter and a brothy, savoury taste known as umami. All other tastes are shades and combinations of these.

EQUALLY there are only seven smells: putrid, pungent, ethereal, minty, floral, musky and camphoric. All other smells are blends, but we can detect at least 10,000 subtle variations, and these can instantly hook up to memories without verbal parts of the brain being involved: granny's house, wet clothes drying on radiators, lawn mowing in summer, a road being tarred, a particular garden shed – whatever you recorded on your nasal playlist perhaps years before. And that's with 40 million receptors. Think what dogs can do with 25 times as many.

BRITISH male stripper Frankie Jakeman's penis is insured for more than both of Dolly Parton's breasts. His organ is valued at £1million while her famous assets are covered at only $600,000 the pair (above). At this price, insurers might be tempted to sew back any valuable detached penis: it worked for John Wayne Bobbitt of Virginia, whose wife famously cut his off in 1993 and threw it from a speeding car, then had regrets and called the police. They searched the roadside, found presumably the right member and had it successfully reattached.

CELEBRITY body part insurance dates back to the 1920s when famously crossed-eye silent movie heartthrob Ben Turpin insured his eyes for $25,000 against their ever uncrossing. Presumably Rod Stewart's insurance of his voice - for an unknown amount - is similarly also against its ever becoming normal, instead of the sandpaper-on-velvet tone which has given him worldwide success.

SOCCER star David Beckham's legs were worth more than twice as much - at £70 million - as Lord of the Dance Michael Flatley's at £35million. It's a far cry from Betty Grable who in the 1940s invented the phrase 'million dollar legs' for insuring her pins for that amount (*each*, as a matter of fact, with Lloyd's of London, although what use one of them would have been in a film is doubtful). Mariah Carey (below) insured her legs for £1billion in 2006.

THE oddest celebrity body part insurance was for taste buds, at $400,000, in a policy taken out by late British food critic Egon Ronay. Any future policies will be taken with a pinch of salt, no doubt.

IF you flattened out the surface of just the small intestine you could carpet a two-storey house with it. A just cut-out tonsil bounces like a rubber ball.

THE loudest yet eructation, or burp as it is commonly known, by Londoner Paul Hunn in 2000, was recorded at 118 decibels, as loud as a jet aircraft taking off. His companions would be legally entitled to ear protectors.

YOUR blood will travel 60,000 miles today, even if you go nowhere.

JUST as there is little evolutionary explanation for laughter, there is absolutely none for yawning. If, as is argued, it replenishes oxygen when we have somehow forgotten to breathe because we are so bored, why do foetuses in the womb yawn, why is it infectious, and why do athletes do it after their warm ups and breathing exercises? People given oxygen in tests yawn more, not less.

A BIZARRE laughing epidemic overtook the Bukoba district of what is now Tanzania in 1962. It affected 95 of the 159 pupils of a school, which was forced to close. This merely spread the problem wider until more than 1,000 people were affected. Scientists took blood samples and searched for a toxic gas or virus that could explain the behaviour. It disappeared as suddenly as it started. Those affected insisted it was not funny.

FEMALE breasts do not legally constitute private parts in Arizona.

YOU could make the 'lead' for 9,000 pencils out of the carbon in your body.

IN Bahrain a male doctor may legally look at a female's genitals but only in a mirror, which must make applying any medication difficult.

FAT CHANCE: In parts of West Africa, the fattest girls are considered the most beautiful; Keira Knightley would be thought super-ugly.

FLIRTING: The origins of flirting are primitive. Men are programmed to find hemispherical female body parts - breasts and buttocks - attractive, because this will most likely produce successful breeding. When a smart lady in a cocktail dress looks across her bare rounded shoulder and makes eye contact, she may think she's being cool and sophisticated, but in primitive terms she's saying: 'I've got working mating equipment. Inseminate me.'

COYNESS: Showing the part of her neck that carries vulnerable arteries, by tilting her head, is a classic animal submission posture, and tilting the wrist coyly to expose a similar danger spot has the same function: I am offering you something better than a quick meal. Laughing at a man's jokes is an evolutionary acknowledgment of his dominance (see, if you doubt it, how funny business executives find their superiors' jokes, and how unfunny their inferiors'). Or, of course, they might actually *be* funny.

MEN who come over all child-like and lovely-dovey with women are saying, knowingly or not, 'I'm checking out whether you are good mother material'. Equally, according to this theory, women find men who can make funny or expressive faces attractive (Mel Gibson, below, for example) because this skill would be needed with infants.

EVEN more bizarre is the reason given by some evolutionists for women's breasts remaining inflated for their whole adult lives, instead of just when rearing infants as with other mammals (who are, after all, defined by this activity). Our African ancestors had to move to become seashore dwellers and swimmers at some point, due to other dangers, and this is when we lost our all-over body hair (compared to apes, who fled to the trees). For reliable reproduction, it was better for the vagina to move forwards so it wasn't constantly in the sand or mud. This made mating from the front necessary. This in turn made inflated breasts an advantage as a buttock substitute for arousing males. It's difficult to prove, but it can't be denied that men (some of them) spend millions on magazines filled with, largely, breasts, and women spend millions of dollars on getting them enlarged, or getting push-up bras and low cut tops, so whatever it is, it's still working.

PUBIC HAIR remains in the area above the genitals because it traps odours necessary for sexual arousal.

ONE reason women are on average 7 per cent shorter than men is to enable them to lie with their noses close to their partners' armpits, (not an advantage, they may feel!). Secretly, nature lets them inhale pheromones released during love-making to trigger ovulation. If this theory, put forward by Desmond Morris, is true, then the decline in western fertility could be traced to the arrival of powerful roll-on deodorants!

GAY men's brains are different to heterosexual men's, a Californian neuroscientist called le Vay (yes, a relation) has found. The difference is in an area of the hypothalamus.

SCATTERING SEED: Men make 100,000 sperm a minute. Chances that any particular sperm will become a child: about 1 in 200 billion - and that's only for a partnered straight guy! Sperm manufacture continues at the same rate no matter how often or rarely a man ejaculates.

EGGSACT TOTAL: Women, on the other hand, make no

eggs after they're born - menopause is when they run out of the ones they were born with. To put it another way, the apparently inherited-from-mother characteristics of a new-born baby weren't fixed in its mother's womb but in its grandmother's womb. So when a woman is pregnant, she is also carrying her future grandchildren (well, the eggs for them), and a woman loses eggs at a rate of far more than the one a month the period would suggest.

MALES are fertile into old age so it should be possible even now to find someone (of either sex) whose grandfather was born in the 18th century. Let's do the maths: woman of 90, born of a father of 65, born of a father of 65 equals 220 years. From 2019, that's back to 1799. With all the billions of people in the world, and fathers of 70 not unknown, it's bound to be possible.

ISAAC NEWTON devised a temperature scale which used 'the armpit temperature of a healthy Englishman' as one of its markers (12 degrees in his scale). You need at least two constant markers to invent such a scale, and this one wasn't as daft as it might first sound – it's a surprisingly steady temperature, while almost everything else seems to change or is difficult to replicate.

He chose the other end as the freezing point of water: boiling water was 34. Fahrenheit, whose scale is in official use in only the USA and four small countries, chose the zero point as the coldest temperature he could produce by mixing ice and certain common chemicals, which gave us the deeply odd situation of anything under +32F being below water's freezing point. Celsius, who eventually invented the centigrade scale we widely use, initially had it completely the other way round - 100 was freezing and 0 was boiling.

MOST people, buildings, works of art, flowers and insects, and even pieces of music considered particularly beautiful contain the Golden Ratio of 1:1.618. It is defined as the proportion from which nothing can be added or subtracted without making it worse. How often do you see a square picture in a magazine or newspaper?

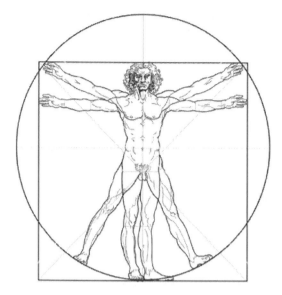

IN people with beautiful figures, take the distance from the soles of the feet to the navel to be 1, that from the feet to the top of the head will be 1.618, as in Leonardo's famous Vitruvian Man drawing. The Golden Ratio also applies to width of nose to width of mouth in Queen Nefertiti, Pierce Brosnan, Marlene Dietrich (below), Marilyn Monroe and many other beauties.

15 Business: Strange company we keep...

MOTORISTS on the A1 trunk road between London and Edinburgh may be forgiven for rubbing their windscreens in disbelief when they spot 'Established 1498' on removal vans. After all, that's so old the firm would have had to wait more than 200 years to move a Queen-Anne chair and three centuries to deliver anything to New Zealand. But Graham Burnett, partner in the world's oldest transport business - still called Aberdeen Shore Porters' Society – said the firm, set up to deal with the harbour's Baltic and Low countries trade, was first mentioned in Aberdeen Council minutes of June 20, 1498.

OLDER still is the Faversham Oyster Fishery Company in Kent, referred to in its own Act of Parliament as existing 'from time immemorial' - i.e. in English law, from before 1189. So there were 717 years to wait before their oysters could be served in The Ritz, which opened in 1906.

AFTER 800 MINTS: The Bank of England was rather pleased with itself in 1994 as it was its 300th anniversary: a commemorative £2 coin was struck, proudly bearing the dates 1694 and 1994. But compared to the makers of the coins - the Royal Mint - the Old Lady of Threadneedle Street, as the Bank is known, was a mere spotty teenager. More than 1,100 years ago, in 886, Alfred the Great occupied London and there was a large issue of silver pennies bearing his portrait and stamped Londonia in a monogram. That was clearly the Royal Mint. And you could claim its origins date as far back as AD287, when a Roman rebel called Carausius started striking his own coins in London. The development of the Royal Mint from a primitive Anglo-Saxon moneyer's workshop to the Mint within the Tower of London, then to the Tower Hill site and finally to a purpose-built plant at Llantrisant in South Wales has been achieved without a break - but with plenty of change.

THE OLDEST continually operating company in the United States still making its original product was started in 1816 when Ilion, New York blacksmith Eliphalet Remington entered a shooting competition with his home-made rifle. Other farmers were so impressed they flocked to place orders, and an industry was born which has since seen the U.S. through the conquest of the Wild West and various wars and is still going with a bang.

STATUS CYMBALS: But if you think that tells you something about Britain and America – that their oldest big companies make money and rifles – then the equivalent American oldest *small* business to the British oyster firm (above) is equally surprising. The cymbal company Zildjian was founded in Constantinople (now Istanbul, Turkey) in 1623 after a man was messing about with alloys trying to make gold and ended up with one that made a nice sound when hit, without breaking. They were used for 200 years by the military to frighten the enemies of the Ottoman empire. The name Zildjian means 'son of the cymbal maker' and eventually the business moved to Massachusetts. They also make drum sticks to hit the things with. If you've listened to music at all in the past 50 years, you'd have heard the products, from Ringo Starr (below) in The Beatles to Tre Cool in Green Day.

THAT a Yorkshire firm is selling baguettes to the French may sound like a 'coals to Newcastle' story, but the achievement is far from unique in the annals of British salesmanship. This follows such coups as the Sussex firm which sells freezers to the Eskimos; the Midlands company sending computers to the Japanese and a Surrey wood-working company which supplies ethnic knick-knacks to souvenir shops around the world, many to be brought back to Surrey. The baguettes, by Foster's bakery in Barnsley, are in the tradition of the Hertfordshire company which earns its crust sells pasta to the Italians; the factory in Sunderland exporting Nissan cars to Japan; the Derbyshire firm exporting banana plants to the Caribbean and the concern in Spalding, Lincolnshire, selling bulbs to Holland. There's even a firm selling sand to the Arabs. It's a special sand, for foundries.

GREAT WRONG PREDICTION *(No 10)!*
An American bank which introduced an early type of ATM (hole-in-the-wall cash) machine invented by Luther George Simjian in 1939 discontinued the experiment because in the bank's opinion an ATM would be used 'only by prostitutes and gamblers who didn't want to deal with tellers face-to-face'.

HOLE IN THE WALL: The first modern ATM machine was launched by British comedian Reg Varney in Enfield, North

London in 1967 but used coded strips of paper you had to buy in advance; the first machine as we know it today by New York's Chemical Bank in 1969.

'ALWAYS the bridesmaid, never the bride' sounds like an ancient folksy wisdom, but it's actually a brilliant bit of advertising writing, for Listerine mouthwash, first appearing in 1925. But that followed a music hall song *Why Am I Always a Bridesmaid* which featured two lines:

> *Why am I always a bridesmaid,*
> *Never the blushing bride?*

The song was written by Fred Leigh who evidently had a theme going here, as he came up with the still familiar *Don't Dilly Dally* and *Waiting at the Church*.

MAKING A PACKET: The longest company name on record was made when the The Isle of Wight Royal Mail Steam Packet Company merged with the Southampton, Isle of Wight & Portsmouth Improved Steamboat Company to create the Southampton, Isle of Wight and South of England Royal Mail Steam Packet Company Ltd in 1861. The company then bought the Bournemouth & South Coast Steam Packets Ltd in 1908, so could have become the Southampton, Isle of Wight, South of England, Bournemouth & South Coast Royal Mail Steam Packet Company Ltd - but took pity on the sign writer and settled for Red Funnel Ferries, which firm still plies the Solent every day.

FAT LOT OF GOOD: The U.S. plus-sized and maternity fashion business Lane Bryant was named by accident when a bank clerk mistyped the name of the founder, Lena Bryant, on her first account. Like the average American woman, the business has grown and grown since being founded in 1904, though slogans such as 'Calling all chubbies' would probably not fit too well today. 'I'm no angel' was a more recent raunchier tagline for its larger lingerie.

COMPANIES whose founders' identities are thinly disguised in their names include (see bold bits) **A**lan **M**ichael **S**ugar **Trad**ing; **GAR**y Burrell and Dr. **MIN** Kao; Ingvar **K**amprad of **E**lmtaryd, **A**gunnaryd; and Harold **MATT** Matson and **EL**liot Handler.

16 Tax: The meaner, or dafter, you still pay

Only two things in life are certain, the sages say, and they're both horrible: Death and taxes. What is less certain is what will be taxed, why, and for how long...

TAX: Was never supposed to be permanent. In Ancient Greece the Athenians taxed people during war, but gave them a refund if the war involved seizing treasure. They also stopped it on the day the war finished.

INCOME TAX was similarly invented by Britain in 1800 for the duration of the Napoleonic Wars with France. Once they were won, the taxes were repealed and all records were supposed to have been burnt. Some were, but secretly the state hung on to the idea.

THE AMERICANS copied the British idea for the War of 1812 – against, ironically, the British – with a progressive income tax, that is one where the poor paid less than 1 per cent and the rich 10 per cent. As the war ended quickly, the tax was scrapped. Similarly an American income tax law of 1861 didn't work. Finally in 1862, because the Civil War was raging, income tax was imposed in the Union. Not everyone took any notice – by 1870, just 276,000 people out of 38 million filed a return.

WINDOW TAX: Going around Britain, you will occasionally see bricked-up windows, results of the notorious Window Tax of 1766 whereby the government charged people for the privilege of seeing God's good light. It was perhaps aimed at the rich who have bigger houses – the Dukes of Devonshire have a 'calendar house' at Chatsworth, that is one room for all 365 days of the year – but in fact *they* could afford it, whereas the very poor who already lived in near darkness suffered more. The 'stopping up' to avoid the tax had to be

with the same material as the wall, which is why you see brick filled with brick (below), stone with stone, etc, to show it was permanent. The mean beggars!

DAFT TAXES: Other taxes have included:

HAT TAX. You had to have a duty stamp on the inside of your hat. Given that everyone wore a hat until World War II, the scope was enormous.

TEA AND COFFEE TAX: These were insanely highly taxed in Britain at certain periods, and this led to smuggling of whatever commodity being taxed. At one point most tea drunk in Britain was smuggled. But since the Starbucks revolution and coffee shops in every street, office, museum, bookshop and garden centre, the Chancellor's arguably missing a trick in not restarting them. On the other hand, don't do it too much - tax on tea was one cause of the American Revolution.

GLOVE TAX was another apparently daft one – again aimed at

the better off. The poor wore rags on their hands, so could, as it were, put two fingers up to glove tax.

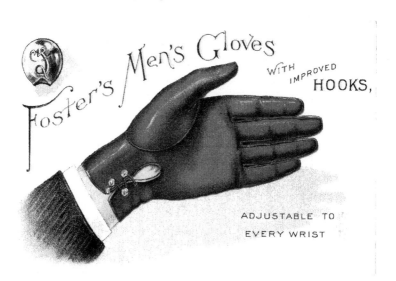

THAT'S RICH: If you tax the rich *less*, you usually get *more* revenue, as former Labour Chancellor Denis Healey now admits (having tried to tax the rich's socks off). The rich aren't stupid – or they employ people who aren't stupid – and they have spare money slopping about which can be put in various tax-avoiding places. Whereas the poor and middling have just enough to live on. If you make tax bearable, the rich don't bother to avoid it. New York billionairess Leona Helmsley famously took this too far with her attitude: 'We don't pay taxes. Only the little people pay taxes.' She was jailed, and died in 2007.

TAX DISASTERS: Many of the disasters between government and the people have been caused by tax, and not just in Britain. For example, England lost France in the 100 Years' War because of resented tax policies. Charles I had his head chopped off because of his hated Ship Tax. The American colonies were lost because of the Sugar Tax, Stamp Tax and tea duty (hence the Boston Tea Party). Salt tax saw the British kicked out of India. Yes, there were other problems, but tax was the common factor.

IT DIDN'T STOP THEM: Once the Americans had kicked out the British in 1783, with the battle cry 'No taxation without representation' you might have thought everything tax-wise would have been hunky-dory. Not a bit of it. Rebellions against unfair taxes took place in 1794 and 1798, then caused friction during the War of 1812. Having kicked out one set of unfair tax imposers, the people were darrned if they were going to let another lot in.

TAX ADDICTS: The government will tax anything that people are addicted to or attracts moral disdain - often the same thing. Thus poor people in Britain who buy cigarettes, lottery tickets, petrol (gasoline), betting slips and booze are paying much more tax proportionately than rich people, who are supposedly taxed at a higher rate. The rich can find things to spend their money on that do not attract tax; even if they smoke, etc, there's only so much one person, billionaire or benefits claimant, can get through, so the tax proportion is tiny. In fact if said poor people live on state benefits, the state gets most of it straight back.

A TAX ON TAX: The British Government even gets away with a tax on a tax. Road fuel is taxed with a heavy duty, then this whole amount is taxed with VAT. The result is that petrol that costs around 25p a litre to reach the pump costs more than four times as much at the time of writing.

HIDDEN TAXES: If you charge a phone company billions of pounds for mobile phone frequencies, they charge twice as much for text messaging. It doesn't *look* like a tax, but is one - again, arguably, on an addiction. Another hidden tax is to charge British train operators a premium of a billion pounds for operating a service. Passengers are paying twice as much for tickets as they should. It doesn't seem like a tax. It is one.

WON'T GO AWAY: Once someone's thought of a tax, it's hard to get rid of it. In Ancient Rome, Caesar Augustus thought of an inheritance tax, with property left to a spouse exempted. It sounds familiar because it's still going.

DAFT TAX YEAR: The reason why Britain's tax year runs to such an eccentric date, April 5 is because in the 18th century the British Julian calendar needed adjusting to the Continental Gregorian one, losing 11 days (see Page 192). The tax man couldn't be bothered to cope with an incomplete year so the tax year ran on from the usual quarter day, March 25 (the year was divided into quarters for rents, etc), and we've been stuck trying to catch up ever since. Perhaps the taxman wants to make a mammoth effort one year but never quite does.

KEEPING TALLY: In medieval England, taxes collected were recorded on a 'tally stick', notches on a stick which could be cut in half lengthways so that both the Government and the probably illiterate taxpayer would have a record or receipt. Any argument, and the two halves could be joined again. Being civil servants, they meticulously filed them away in bundles under the Palace of Westminster for nigh on a thousand years.

DELETING THE RECORDS: Eventually, in 1834, someone decided the tally sticks (above) would not be needed to settle 800-year-old tax disputes. Charles Dickens retold what happened: 'It would naturally occur to any intelligent person that nothing could be easier than to allow them to be carried away for firewood by the miserable people who live in that neighbourhood. However, they never had been useful, and official routine required it that they never should be, and so the order went forth that they should be privately and confidentially burned.' Civil servants again.

The sticks were confidential documents so ordinary people couldn't be allowed to see one, even 800 years later. The burning in a furnace under the House of Lords soon spread to the mountains of crisp, centuries-old sticks all around. Parliament burned down that night, October 16, 1834, achieving what Guy Fawkes had failed to do with the Gunpowder Plot of November 5, 1605. That's the real reason why we have the sublime gothic masterpiece that is today's Houses of Parliament: massive tax cock-ups.

OBSCURE OBSOLETE OBELISKS: Talking about burning things down, the Great Fire of London of 1666 led to a tax that carried on centuries too long. The Coal and Wine Dues put a levy on every ton of coal and barrel of wine heading for the capital at a point on entry routes. These paid for Wren's superb set of City churches, including St Paul's, to replace those burnt down. The trouble was that the tax carried right through the 18th century and halfway through the 19th, when hundreds of cast iron obelisks were still being erected beside every road, canal and railway leading into the capital to show where the tax was due. Today few people know why they are there (showing the City's red cross with a dagger, below), except that they were also used to mark the Metropolitan Police boundary.

PLAYING CARD TAX: The Ace of Spades is the harbinger of death, as recounted on Page 8, because there was a government tax or duty on playing cards. From 1765, the duty paid became noted on the Ace of Spades, which was therefore printed in a fantastical and elaborate manner, to avoid forgeries, and still is the most complex in any pack. The penalty for forging an ace of spades was death, a sentence carried out at least once, in 1805. The duty on playing cards, which had then been reduced to 3d, was stopped only as recently as 1967.

17 How crime & punishment can be strangely funny

NOOSE-FLASH: Newspaper stories about hangings of criminals are nearly always accompanied by pictures of a noose with the familiar coiled hangman's knot (below left). Boy Scouts and other youngsters have always found that famous knot a subject of macabre fascination. Punctilious players of the spelling game Hangman always take delight in drawing such a noose at the critical stage. Yet the hangman's knot, or indeed any knot, was not used by British executioners - certainly not for the last 150 years of hanging until it was abolished in 1964.

The rope (a used one below right) used had a large brass eye spliced in at one end, and a small one at the other. The small one was passed through the large, forming the noose, and then attached to a shackle on a chain over the beam of the gallows, allowing the drop to be adjusted so that the neck was efficiently broken, avoiding the extremes of the head being pulled off by too great a drop, or of slow strangulation with too short a one.

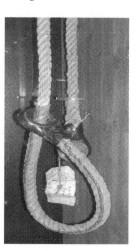

175

NOT A KNOT: On whose word should we base such a surprising claim (above)? That of a member of the most famous family of British executioners, Albert Pierrepoint, who wrote in 1931 in his notes on execution procedures for Pentonville prison: 'There is no knot. That fancy cowboy coil of a "hangman knot" is something we abandoned to the Americans 100 years ago. In Britain the rope runs free through a pear-shaped metal eye woven into the rope's end, and the operative part of the noose is covered with soft wash leather.' He added concerning the hangman's knot: '…it eventually kills by suffocation. Leave that to the Americans.' Several sources attest to the British habit of placing chamois leather at the 'operative part' of the noose. This was (as mentioned above) to prevent rope burns on the neck of the person being hanged, an odd consideration for someone you are trying to kill, and particularly so because, if the hanging was as efficient as claimed, any sensation of being burned would hardly have time to register.

CRIMINAL STUPIDITY: Don't we all love it when stupid criminals incriminate themselves? Before they even get to court sometimes. In **Boulder, Colorado**, a man who denied being anywhere near an armed robbery complained: 'The officer can't have recognised me, because I had a ski mask at the robbery.'

In **Perth, Scotland,** a man arrested after a burglary said on record: 'I don't know anything about stolen pearl necklaces.' Neither did the police. They went and checked with the householder, who then found they were indeed missing.

The **English robber** who pulled down his balaclava helmet over his eyes only to find it had no eye holes, being a woolly hat, and blundered around the shop he was trying to rob, crashing into things until caught. The **Irish thief** who suggested a post master who didn't have enough money write him a cheque – made payable to his own name.

Or the **Miami** factory break-in villain who tried to run away from police in darkened streets – wearing those trainers that flash brightly every time you step.

And then there's the court preliminaries. A **Texas** defendant strenuously denied manufacturing the drug methamphetamine,

and asked for an appointed attorney. The judge asked the usual questions about whether this person needed this kind of legal aid.
Judge: Mr Jones, how long have you been in custody?
Jones: A month and a half.
Judge: What did you do before you were incarcerated?
Jones: I manufactured methamphetamine.

HANGING AROUND THE BAR: Albert Pierrepoint (above) said somewhat chillingly: 'Hanging must run in the blood' as his father and uncle were hangmen. He kept a pub called, somewhat bizarrely, given his profession, Help The Poor Struggler. He executed all 15 spies hanged during the Second World War and several drinkers reported that at his final pub in Hoole, Lancs, there was a sign 'No hanging around the bar', which he, always reluctant to discuss his other job, later denied. He died in 1992. In bed.

SPEED CAMERAS: Are not usually funny. But one motorist in a West London suburb was snapped by a speed camera and police sent him the usual picture of his car speeding and a demand for £60. The motorist sent them a photograph of £60 in notes. However he paid up pretty quick when police replied with a picture of handcuffs.

SCAPEGALLOWS: John 'Babbacombe' Lee, 'the man they could not hang', was convicted of the brutal murder of his employer, an elderly spinster, who had her throat cut in Babbacombe, Devon, in November 1884. A failed attempt to burn the house down and cover up the crime followed.

Lee denied the killing but was convicted on circumstantial evidence, and sentenced to hang in February 1885, at Exeter Prison. The hangman tested the trap door, which worked perfectly. The noose was put on Lee, who stood on it, and the hangman pulled the lever. Nothing happened. It had never jammed before. Lee was removed, the thing adjusted by a carpenter, tested again, and 20 minutes later the lever was pulled and again nothing happened. A third time this process was followed, with a plane used to make plenty of clearance for the trapdoor, but

there was still no hanging. It is traditional that after three attempts, a person cannot be executed (although this is the only known example with trapdoor hangings).

The hangman was clearly distressed and refused to eat his hearty breakfast, which Lee gladly wolfed down (none, of course, had been provided for him).

Home Secretary Sir William Harcourt commuted the death sentence to life penal servitude, saying: 'It would shock the feeling of anyone if a man had twice to pay the pangs of imminent death.' Odd thing to say. Lee had to face it *three* times. And does one pay pangs?

Lee (pictured) was released in 1907, and fled to the United States. There was still no proof that he committed the crime. But he wasn't hanging around for someone to find out...

Lee, the 'man they could not hang'

18 Laws: So daft, they should be illegal

IT IS illegal for a cab in the City of London to carry rabid dogs or corpses, or for persons to hail a cab while having the plague.

ON the other hand it is legal for a cab driver to urinate on the rear offside wheel, if he keeps his right hand on the bodywork. Presumably he needs his other hand, and it rather suggests the law was framed before women drove London cabs.

HACKNEY carriages - that is taxis - in London are legally obliged, or were until recently, to carry a bale of hay on the roof.

IT IS illegal to die in the Houses of Parliament. People are carried out and declared dead outside the premises. Disneyland follows a similar regime.

EASTER, falling as it does at unpredictable times, is illegal in Britain. The Easter Act 1928 which passed into law prescribes that Easter Day will be the Sunday following the second Saturday in April. This was to include the entire British Empire and the Irish Free State. It has never been enforced, with Easter instead following an insanely complex formula involving the Golden Numbers and the Pope, so it can fall in March. As the Eastern church didn't reform its calendar at the same time as the Roman church, Easter can fall differently in both halves of Christianity, both unpredictable by any logical rules. And still illegal in Britain.

BRITAIN is the only country that legally doesn't have to state its name on its stamps. All British stamps must bear the image of the monarch, even if only in the corner. King George V loved nothing better than getting on his hands and knees and filling his stamp album - mostly, it must be said,

with pictures of himself (below) or his close relatives. Talking to His Majesty about stamps was a good move, because philately will get you everywhere.

IT IS forbidden to call a pig Napoleon in France, which may be why George Orwell did call a pig by that name in Animal Farm.

IN Calgary, Alberta, Canada, every business establishment must, according to law, have hitching posts outside. Anyone ejected from the city is entitled to a horse and a day's worth of rations.

ROYAL NAVY ships that enter the Pool of London - that is the bit between Tower Bridge and London Bridge - must by law provide a barrel of rum to the Constable of the Tower of London. And they do.

IN BRITAIN, a pregnant woman can legally urinate wherever she wants - even, if she so requests, in a policeman's helmet.

IT IS against the law in Britain (Malicious Damage Act 1861) maliciously to destroy or damage any book kept for the purpose of science, art or literature. Playwright Joe Orton was prosecuted under this law for putting rude captions in Islington library books in 1962. Later his co-defendant maliciously destroyed Orton's brain with a hammer.

THE death penalty applies, according to a law signed by Henry III, to anyone wounding, maiming or killing fairies.

IT IS illegal in England to eat a mince pie (below) on Christmas Day. This was a law enacted by the Puritans during the Commonwealth of the 17th century and never repealed.

DANCING round maypoles was also banned, as were maypoles themselves, which were chopped down and burnt (so Mayfair in London became purely residential, for example). It was never firmly established whether these laws, not signed by a King, were legal after the Restoration of the Monarchy. Some were applied, and some weren't.

GERMAN farmers must spend at least 20 seconds every day with each pig, 10 seconds in the morning and 10 seconds in the afternoon, says a 2002 law.

IN England, all men aged 17-60 must carry out two hours of longbow practice a week. Unless they are lame, maimed or decrepit, a priest, or a baron, or all of those things. In fact until around 1966, all other sports were illegal for this reason, except for noblemen worth more than £100 a year, and only within their property. In Scotland, golf was similarly banned to encourage archery practice. Golfers fled to the coast and thus 'links' courses were first formed. (Source: Unlawful Games Act 1541). Links meant dunes.

IN London, Freemen of the City of London are legally allowed to take a flock of sheep across London Bridge without being charged a toll, or being prevented; they are also allowed to drive geese down Cheapside. The former has been implemented recently, to the great consternation of police.

ALSO in London, it is illegal to roll any cask, tub, hoop or wheel on any footway, except for unloading any cart. The same 1839 Metropolitan Police Act bans places for 'fighting or baiting of lions, bears, badgers, cocks' with a fine up to £5.

ALL peers entering Oakham, England must present a horseshoe to Oakham castle. This even applies to royalty, with the Prince of Wales being a recent donor (2003) while the oldest dated horseshoe hanging in the castle is from 1470. But it applies only on their first visit. It would apply to the Queen if she visited. This small town bizarrely has its own county council, Rutland (abolished and then recreated in recent decades), its symbol being, yes, the horseshoe.

GIPSIES were banned by the Egyptians Act of 1530 - they were thought wrongly to have come from Egypt, hence the name - and ordered to go 'back' there or at least leave the country within 15 days. They didn't. This was amended in 1554 to letting them stay if the quit their 'naughty, idle and ungodly life' (which could cover quite a lot of other people nowadays who should also be wrongly sent to Egypt, you may well feel). Come to think of it, if they came from India as their language suggests, they deserved the title 'Indians' more than the Indians in North America, who didn't.

IN Lancashire, you are not permitted to incite a dog to bark on the seashore, after being asked to stop by a constable to desist.

IN Chester, Welshmen are banned from entering the city before sunrise and from staying after sunset. It is legal to kill a Welshman after dark in that city with a crossbow at a range of 12 yards; similarly it is legal to kill a Scotsman in York if said Scot is carrying a bow and arrows. Leaving aside the morality of taking these old laws seriously, it is unlikely that other laws would not come into play.

THE reigning monarch must stop at the Temple Bar (an old gate) in Fleet Street and ask the Lord Mayor for permission to enter the City of London. Even though the Temple Bar has long gone.

IT is illegal under the California Alcoholic Beverage Control Act for producers of alcoholic drinks to list the names of retailers or restaurants that sell their products in advertising or even in newsletters.

ANY sturgeon fish caught in British waters must be offered to the monarch under a 1324 law. A West Country fisherman fell foul of this in 2004. Doesn't apply to politician Nicola Sturgeon.

WEARING armour to Parliament is illegal (1279 law, based on royal prerogative). In the House of Commons, MPs must keep behind the line on the floor on their side - to keep them a sword's length apart - hence 'toeing the line'.

BEING drunk in charge of a road-going steam engine makes you liable to a £200 fine or 51 weeks in jail (Licensing Act 1872). Such an engine may not pull more than one wagon over the bridge at Henley-on-Thames, signs still warn you. A sign on a bridge at Wareham in Dorset (below) threatens to transport you to Australia if you damage it. Bonzer bargain, cobber!

METHUSELAHS, Salamanazars, Balthazars or even Nebuchadnezzars, the traditional very large and extreme champagne bottle sizes, are all illegal in Florida, if you're planning to celebrate there.

IN El Salvador, drunk drivers can be punished by death before a firing squad. In China a firing squad can charge the condemned person for the bullets. They have been known to avoid aiming at areas wanted for transplant.

OSCAR WILDE was famously imprisoned in 1895 with hard labour for his then illegal homosexual affair. But the law in question was, bizarrely, 'An Act to make further provision for the Protection of Women and Girls.'

ON Sark, the tiny Channel island said to be the last feudal state in Europe, only the Dame of Sark, or Seigneur if a man, may keep a bitch. Each tenement (land-holding), which can never be divided by inheritance or divorce, must if required supply one musket for the island's defence.

IN Vermont, women according to law must obtain written permission from their husbands to wear false teeth. In Florida, unmarried women who parachute on Sundays can be imprisoned.

THE head of any dead whale found on the British coast is legally the property of the King; the tail, on the other hand, belongs to the Queen - in case she needs the bones for her corset. Source: 1324 royal prerogative.

ALL swans in Britain are Royal birds and belong to the Queen. There are heavy penalties for harming them: A year and day's jail for stealing a swan's egg, and if one is killed, the miscreant must pour sufficient grain on the dead swan, hung from a ceiling vertically, to cover it completely.

IT IS legal under a 540-year-old law for a person with land worth four marks to own a swan on totally enclosed water (ie a pond) on his land. Whatever four marks are.

THE exception is some birds owned by the Companies of Dyers & Vintners in the City on the Thames, under a 1473 law. The Queen's Swan Marker, in a complex ceremony

known as Swan Upping (pictured), must lead six boats up the river each year to mark the offspring of each lot of birds, the Dyers' birds get one nick in their beaks and the Vintners' get two nicks, punched out rather as railway tickets used to be punched by inspectors, and the Queen's get none. It takes several weeks and is all completely pointless.

IN Chicago, it is illegal to eat in a place that is on fire.

IN Lehigh, Nebraska, it is forbidden to sell doughnut holes. This isn't quite as mad as it sounds, because they are small pieces of cooked pastry made from the material punched from ring doughnuts.

ALSO in Nebraska, it is illegal to sell beer without soup brewing; to sleep naked in a hotel even if married, or to burp in church (even for children, whose parents would be arrested).

ON the Isle of Man, not legally part of England, although once part of Norway, no laws were written down until 1417 as they were said to be 'locked up in the breasts of the Deemsters' who were judges, one for the north and one for the south. Cynics thought this 'breast law' was just made up as they went along.

THE Deemsters still exist. Their oath said: 'I do swear that I will execute the laws of the isle justly betwixt party and party as indifferently as the herring's backbone doth lie in the midst of the fish.' Or, as visiting Cockneys would put it, so you won't get done up like a kipper.

ACCORDING to the Town Police Clauses Act, 1847, hanging washing in the street, beating a carpet before 8am, or flying a kite is illegal in British towns, and liable for a 40 shilling fine. Beating doormats is legal, however, at any time.

NO Jew or Roman Catholic who becomes British Prime Minister can advise on the choice of bishops and archbishops in the Churches of England, Ireland or Scotland. But an atheist, a Buddhist, a Muslim, a Hindu or a Jedi (religion) *can* (Roman Catholic Relief Act, 1829, and Jews Relief Act, 1858).

NO member of the British Royal Family who is under 25 may marry without the permission of the Monarch: this law was used to stop the romance of Princess Margaret with Group Captain Peter Townsend, because he was divorced. The marriage of the Prince of Wales who became George IV to Catholic widow Mrs Fitzherbert in 1795 was declared illegal under the same law. It is a crime to assist in such a marriage. (BTW, in order to carry on with this dowdy older woman George IV slighted his much prettier real wife whom the people loved. She died young, resulting in an emotional funeral procession through Kensington. Sounds familiar?)

THAT previous Act is incorporated in Canadian law. German descendants of the Dukes of Hanover still have to apply for permission to marry from the Queen of England - if they want to be considered legally married in Britain and the Commonwealth.

IF you are owed £1 in England, you cannot legally accept 95p in settlement. Mr Justice Kessell in the High Court: 'A creditor can accept anything to settle a debt, except a lesser amount of money. He might take a horse, or a canary, or a tomtit if he chose, and that was accord and satisfaction; but, by a most extraordinary peculiarity of English Common Law, he could not take 19s 6d in the pound, that was *nudum pactum'*. That is a naked pact or one-sided contract - illegal.

BUT in Scotland, naked pacts are OK (naked Picts are another matter) so 25p in the £1 would be legal, if agreed by both sides. So much for supposed Scottish meanness.

THE lovers of Diana, Princess of Wales, should have been burnt at the stake. Under the Treason Act 1351, death is the penalty for anyone who 'do violate the king's companion, or the king's eldest daughter unmarried, or the wife of the king's eldest son.' This last clause covered Diana, who died in that infamous car crash in 1997. The ancient death penalty wasn't abolished until the following year.

BRITISH people cannot die at the same time, legally - for instance in a car crash of husband and wife, it is deemed that the older one died first, for inheritance purposes. But a French couple can die at the same time but are treated as if the other didn't exist. In the case of a factor that would prolong one life, for example a boat sinks and both drown but only one could swim, this doesn't apply, so inheritance goes from one to the other. Briefly.

'TIME IMMEMORIAL' in English law has a precise meaning: i.e. from before 1189. So a precisely dated 1188 thing dates from time immemorial, 'when memory runneth not to the contrary', etc. For example, the Faversham Oyster Fishery Company in Kent is referred to in its own Act of Parliament as existing 'from time immemorial'.

IN Wales in former times, you could keep any house you had started to build at sundown if by sunrise you had the roof on and smoke coming from the chimney. Obviously it had to be on vacant land, of which there was plenty. You could also keep and fence the land around it as far as you could throw an axe. Although most of these 'Ty Un Nos' houses fell down because of being built in a hurry, or were incorporated gradually into proper houses, there is one on the A5 at Capel Curig called the Ugly House, clearly built out of rough boulders.

ANYONE taking sheep, lambs or hogs up College Road in suburban Dulwich, London, must pay 2 1/2 old pence (one modern penny) per score (20). Charged 'in proportion but not less than 1/2d for any less number'. The money must go to Edward Alleyn's College of God's Gift nearby, better known as Dulwich College. The good news is that a return journey on the same day is free.

IT is illegal on Christ Church Meadow in Oxford to partake of kite flying, bowling of hoops, throwing balls, shooting arrows or firing guns and pistols.

IN Britain if you run over a dog you have to stop and tell the owner. If you run over a cat, you can keep going.

IN West Virginia if you run over an animal, you can take it home and eat it for dinner, according to a 1998 law that was supposed to save the state the expense of clearing dead animals from the road. Or, if road kill cuisine becomes popular, could people could start swerving toward animals rather than avoiding them?

IN THE 17TH century, any pigeon poo from British pigeon lofts or dovecotes belonged to the King. Why did he want this vile smelling stuff, too strong to put on crops? It was a vital ingredient in making gunpowder.

A 1925 law in Turkey made it compulsory to wear Panama hats, in a bid to outlaw the traditional Fez.

IT IS illegal to have a sleeping donkey in your bathtub in Oklahoma.

ONE may not legally look miserable in public in Milan. Or be fat in public in Japan.

19 Calendar: Why dates are dangerous

CALENDARS, outwardly harmless, are extremely dangerous, if you try to change them, as it often goes with millions of deaths. Cranks, tyrants, the vain and the revolutionary have tried to impose new calendars on people over the centuries, the Cambodian concept of Year Zero in 1975 typically coinciding with massacres. Tyranny over dates seems to go with tyranny over people.

THE FRENCH REVOLUTIONARY CALENDAR, despite having ten days a week, was not very decimal in having 12 months. The months were *Vendémiaire* (vintage) starting Sept 22, 23 or 24, *Brumaire* (misty), *Frimaire* (frosty), *Nivôse* (snowy), *Pluviôse* (rainy), *Ventôse* (windy), *Germinal* (seed sprouting), *Floréal* (flowering), *Prairial* (meadow), *Messidor* (harvest), *Thermidor* (heat), and *Fructidor* (fruitful). As there were exactly 30 days in each month, the calendar didn't work (none do, because years, months and days do not fit, so they require leap days, etc, but this was worse than normal).

The French bunged six *sans culottides* (days for those without breeches, literally, but days for radicals in a political sense) on the end of the year as holiday, called Day of Genius, Day of the Revolution, etc. The ten-day weeks had one rest day, as do seven-day weeks, so the main point was to con workers into working longer.

As France had until then enjoyed saints' days, every single day of the year was given a new special name - eg the 12th of *Frimaire* was the *Jour de Raifort* (Horseradish day) and the 30th of Ventose was the *Jour de Plantoir* (Dibber Day). No one could remember very many of these, however.

In France the tyrants took this all enormously seriously while chopping people's heads off, while in England - guess what - the French calendar was roundly mocked by calling the Revolutionary months: Wheezy, Sneezy and Freezy; Slippy,

Drippy and Nippy; Showery, Flowery and Bowery; Wheaty, Heaty and Sweety. These may in turn have led to the dwarf names in *Snow White*. In the end Napoleon had had enough and banned it in 1805, only for it to reappear during the Paris Commune of 6-23 May 1871 (or 16 Floréal-3 Prairial An LXXIX as they would put it). Briefly.

THE WORLD IS YOUR LOBSTER: The Zola novel *Germinal*, the *Floreal* class frigates in the French Navy and lobster *Thermidor* all takes their names from French revolutionary months.

THE SOVIET UNION tried to impose a revolutionary calendar from 1929, with five-day weeks, and then from 1931 a six-day week. Efficiency was supposed to rise as there would be rotating rest days for different workers. In fact some took that day off *and* the old Sunday. Again it went with a great slaughter of the people and tyranny. In 1940 it was all scrapped.

ON JANUARY 6 excited children wake up and race to open their Christmas presents. Well they do if they live on Foula, a remote Scottish isle where they celebrate what they consider the real Christmas Day. It's all to do with the 18th century calendar change. Britain skipped 11 days to catch up with Europe's Gregorian calendar (and some people thought 11 days had been stolen from their lives and rioted). Nobody told Foula, between Orkney and the Shetlands, or maybe they didn't agree. The calendar change is also the reason why Britain's tax year runs to such an absurd date (see Page 1731). But then how can *Inland* Revenue stretch to Foula?

20 Obsolete technology lives on, and on ...

IN TV shows, an idea that is abandoned is accompanied by a ripping sounds of a needle being dragged across a vinyl LP record, although no one under 30 has experienced such a moment. Or, probably, even seen such a machine.

WHY are we still invited to 'dial' a phone number or 'ring' someone? What *dial*? Bells used to *ring*, but phones now trill, squeak, warble, play a tune or bleep.

BIG floodlights being switched on, inside buildings or outside, are accompanied on films by a kind of dramatic clanking noise associated with a kind of switchgear that hasn't been used for 80 years. It's all silent.

FLASH photography, eg outside a court room, is accompanied in movies by explosions of one-shot glass bulbs (below) even though these weren't used after electronic flashguns arrived in the 1960s. Equally modern interior scenes of celebs being 'papped' are accompanied by 80s-style motor drive noises on cameras making that zip-zip-zip noise. There's no film to drive as cameras are now digital. Some cameras make a shutter noise even though there is no mechanical shutter, so you know it's working.

FLASH powder in trays once really did create an explosion, BTW, as recreated here. Probably not that handy for a selfie!

IN Britain, trains have *guards*, *coaches* or *carriages*, even though these were horse-drawn stagecoach terms. Equally you can reserve a seat 'facing the engine'. When did you last see a locomotive at the front of a train? If they do have them, they are equally likely to be pushing from the back.

FIGHTERS in space war films swoosh by with a fighter jet noise and look suitably streamlined. In fact they would be silent and brick shaped, needing no streamlining or wings. Explosions would be silent too. They are recreating World War II dogfights.

LIGHT sabres are equally ridiculous. If you have light, you can point it where you like. Unless you are actually trying to recreate fighting with metal swords…

WE describe a room or house as 'well lit'. Nobody lit anything, they just turned switches on. We once *lit* oil, gas and candles.

PEOPLE talk about 'gas boilers' in their homes. If they did boil, they might blow up. People used to boil washing in coppers 100 years ago.

WE 'iron' clothes. What iron? They'd rust if they were, and stain the clothes. Although our great-grandparents once put an iron lump on the range, the electric devices have always been other metals. Equally, when Britons 'put' the kettle 'on', it once meant *on* the range, although nearly everyone uses electric kettles.

SOLDIERS play Russian roulette in movies but – as one tragic real life Mid-Western young man discovered in the 1980s – with automatic weapons, even just one bullet will always be fired. It pushes it to the top of the magazine. You need a revolver, which armies don't use. No, you *don't* need one…

PHONE numbers in Hollywood films always begin 555 although no such exchange exists in any American city. In fact that's exactly *why* it doesn't exist.

21 Names: What's odd about Wendy, Pamela, Thugs and Toerags?

MAKE FRIENDS WITH A THUG: Races, tribes or groups of people who have become, fairly or not, characteristics to the point where the originals are often forgotten include *Thugs, Assassins, Zealots, Vandals, Toerags, Chavs, Philistines,* and *Amazons.* Vikings, however, were *not* a group and should perhaps be written vikings, as it was a Scandinavian word for pirates, not a race. Oddly, they were actually quite civilised by the standards of the day and given the chance would settle down and be peaceful - for example setting up the world's first parliament in the Isle of Man, or founding Dublin.

ZEALOTS were Jewish terrorists (or freedom fighters, depending on your viewpoint) during the Roman Empire. They would hang around public places such as markets with hidden daggers and strike down those they thought were collaborators with the Roman authorities. After an uprising in which they seized Jerusalem, the Zealots ended up besieged by the Romans at Masada and committed mass suicide rather than surrender.

ASSASSINS were a Muslim sect originating in Egypt in about 1090. Persecuted as infidels, they sent suicide killers to combat the dominant Sunnis. According to one theory, the name is linked to hashish, a drug they used in their rites.

THUGS, or Thugees, in 18th century India used to befriend travellers and then later kill them, strangling them and throwing their bodies down wells.

TOERAGS is a British low-level affectionate insult for someone otherwise called a ruffian, urchin or chav. But it probably comes – wrongly - from Tuareg, a tribal group in the Sahara.

CHAV: Another British minor insult for someone ill-educated with bad taste and lots of showy jewellery. It may be (wrongly) connected with *chavvies*, a romany word for children. This language is still spoken by gipsies, a race so-called by Elizabethans because they were supposed to come from Egypt (see Page 183).

MORE MEMORABLE: Stars of stage or screen sometime change their names a little to make them more memorable. So Amelia Driver became **Minnie Driver**. Or Susan Weaver became the far more interesting **Sigourney Weaver.** **Omar Sharif** was Michael Shalhoub. Eileen Regina Edwards became **Shania Twain**. David Williams became **David Walliams.**

OR LESS MEMORABLE (or rather more easily pronounced by more people) **Alan Alda** was Alphonso Joseph D'Abruzzo; **Woody Allen** was Allen Stewart Konigsberg; **Fred Astaire** was Frederick Austerlitz; **Ginger Rogers** was Virginia Katherine McMath; **Lauren Bacall** was Betty Joan Perske; **Dirk Bogarde** was Derek van den Bogaerde.

LESS SILLY: Or the adjustment can be because the original name could be judged by some, far less charitable than ourselves obviously, as downright silly. The singer **Dido**'s real name is Florian Cloud De Bounevialle Armstrong. **Big Daddy**, the hulking 28-stone British wrestling star of the 1960-70s (pictured next page), was really called Shirley Crabtree. Really! He was named after his father who in turn had been named by his 22-stone music hall star mother after the heroine of a Bronte novel before she knew the baby's sex. **Sir Michael Caine** was Maurice Joseph Micklewhite; **Diana Dors** was Diana Mary Fluck. **Colonel Tom Parker** (Elvis's manager) was Andreas Cornelius van Kuijk.

MORE SILLY: Or they can be changed from something a little

dull, although this can sometimes end up too pretentious. The late **L'Wren Scott** (Mick Jagger's other half for many years) was originally called Laura Bambrough. Or someone called Nigel Davies who discovered the early supermodel **Twiggy** (real name Lesley Hornby, pictured below) in the 1960s called himself Justin de Villeneuve. What a nerve, more like.

CELEBS sometimes inflict bizarre names on their offspring. Actor **Forest Whitaker** and his spouse have named their children **Sonnet, True, Ocean** and **Autumn** (they've probably twigged there's a link between Forest and Autumn); musician **Frank Zappa's** children included **Dweezil** and **Moon Unit,** while TV presenter and pop star consort **Paula Yates's** children were so oddly named that after her drug-linked death, cruel Londoners joked: 'Did you know that Lysergic Acid Diethylamide was found beside her bed? But the other children were round at Bob's.' Her children by Bob Geldof were **Fifi-Trixibelle, Peaches** and **Pixie**, and with **Michael Hutchence, Heavenly Hiraani Tiger Lily**. Of this tribe, Yates, Hutchence and Peaches all met early deaths.

PAST SECRETS: It was sometimes thought that asking Briton **Ben Kingsley** to play Gandhi in the Attenborough blockbuster of that name was an odd choice. But then he was born Krishna Bhanji in Scarborough, Yorkshire, England, so maybe not.

SINGERS probably just want to sound nice and positive. **Elaine Paige** was Elaine Bickerstaff. **Dusty Springfield** was Mary Isabel Catherine Bernadette O'Brien, considerably more difficult to get on a 7-inch record label. **Barry Manilow** was Barry Alan Pinkus. English pop star **Adam Faith** started life as Terence Nelhams-Wright. **Bob Dylan** as Robert Zimmerman. **Cliff Richard** as Harry Rodger Webb.

ELTON AND MICK: Unlike his fellow musical knight Sir **Elton John** (real name Reg Dwight) Sir **Mick Jagger's** original name was … Mick Jagger. Don't mess around with something good. Equally, **Prince** was christened Prince.

FILM HEROES: The all-American debonair, virile but suave hero **Cary Grant** (above left) was in fact originally an Englishman called Archibald Leach. Even more ridiculous, archetypal tough guy **John Wayne** (above right) was called Marion Morrison. And for a superpatriot who made so-many pro-American war films, Wayne was strangely backward about volunteering for service in World War II, which he avoided, while fellow stars rushed to the colours after Pearl Harbor. In fact his own wife wrote that he made all the patriotic films later 'trying to atone for staying home'. When his hand prints were put in the pavement in Hollywood, the sand was brought from

Iwo Jima, which Wayne had celebrated in his heroic film, *Sands of Iwo Jima*. The truth is that while his compatriots' blood was seeping into that sand in terrible quantities, he was having a swell time at home. Not quite as brave as his roles...

APT NAMES: Alert British TV viewers noticed recently that a spokesman for water consumers on a recent news programme was a Mr **Fishpool**, who thus joins *Gardeners' Question Time* presenters Pippa **Greenwood** and Bob **Flowerdew** in the happy aptness of their names. But professions being eponymous not anonymous is not confined to television. The list of such stars of nomenclature goes back through Essex music teacher **G. Sharpe**, Hertfordshire dentist **Mr Paine**, Portsmouth choreographer Marilyn **Shufflebottom**, Norfolk sewerage chief Mr **Smellie**, Bedfordshire police crime fighter Sergeant **Lawless**, a poacher from that county **A. Rabbit,** Norfolk policeman **A. Crook,** right back to a Victorian sanitary engineer with a famously rudely suitable name, **Crapper**. The woman in charge of PR for Durex condoms in France was Cecile **Hardon**, while going back a while the man in charge when canal tunnels were put through high ground was, of course, Mr **Underhill**, the patron of early ones with his name on bridges being called the Earl of **Bridgewater**. And in 2008 the man in charge of gritting roads against ice in the North of England was Mr **Skidmore**.

GOOD IF YOU'RE A SYPHILITIC NEEDLE-MAKER: You could always choose a child's name by the relevant saint. The patron saint of needlemakers is St Pancras; of pin makers - St Sebastian (appropriately, given his method of death, pierced by arrows); of tax collectors - St Matthew; of syphilitics - St George; of miners - St Barbara; of cobblers - St Crispin (as featured in Henry V's great speech in the Shakespeare play); of blacksmiths - St Clement (because he was tied to an anchor and thrown in the sea).

BACK TO APT NAMES, or the alleged tendency to follow a career that fits your name, known as nominative determinism, there's a couple of incontinence researchers called **Splatt and Weedon** (British Journal of Urology), the polar researcher

Daniel **Snowman**, the TV weather girl Sara **Blizzard** (East Midlands Today), in the courts **Judge Judge** and **Judge Laws** in England, lawyer **Sue Yoo,** and in America Republicans who argued against action on the ozone layer, **Doolittle** and **Delay**. The British head of French dairy firm Danone in 2010 was Bruno **Fromage**, and don't forget the Belgian footballer who usually plays in the defence, **Mark De Man**. He does indeed.

AN ABSOLUTE goldmine for apt names is the American Directory of Physicians where one researcher pointed out you could find a dermatologist named Dr Rash, a rheumatologist called Dr Knee, an orthopaedic surgeon called Dr Bone and the psychiatrist, Dr Couch. Doctors include 18 doctors called Dr Doctor, 10 named Dr Blood, 19 named Dr Fix, Cure or Heal, and 65 named Dr Flesh, Gore, Ache or Looney. Perhaps not as off-putting – totally wrongly, of course - as the Dr De'Ath or Dr Coffin.

HUNGRY FOR MUSIC: Were children born in the war years fixated on food? You'd think so from the band names chosen by pop and rock stars born in just 1944: Eric Bloom of *Blue Oyster Cult*; Henry Vestine of *Canned Heat*; Gene Parsons of the *Flying Burrito Brothers*; Jack Casady of *Hot Tuna*; John Sebastian of *Lovin' Spoonful*; Edgar Froese of *Tangerine Dream*; Tim Bogert of *Vanilla Fudge*.

WENDY AND PAMELA have a lot in common. They were both names created for books – **Wendy** for *Peter Pan* (1904) and **Pamela** not, as commonly thought, in *Pamela, or Virtue Rewarded* by Richardson (1740) but by Sir Philip Sidney in *Arcadia*, (1590). Also created by writers: **Vanessa** (Jonathan Swift), **Gloria** (Shaw, 1898). Shakespeare invented many, including **Miranda, Jessica** and **Olivia**.

RACE WINNER: British motor racing hero **Sir Stirling Moss** would have been Stirling Moses if his recent ancestors hadn't changed the family name to fit in better. This was common in immigration at the time; comedian **Ben Elton** would have been Ben Ehrenberg. His uncle, Gottfried Ehrenberg, changed his name to Geoffrey Elton only when he joined the British Army in 1944 (rather understandable at the time!). Sir Geoffrey became an ardent Tory, unlike his nephew. Comedian **Sacha Baron Cohen** would have been Sacha Cohen. Sometimes the East European names were so difficult for the Brits to pronounce – looking like the last line of an optician's test card, one joked – that they just picked up a telephone directory on arrival and plumped for a simple name at random. One family thus ended up with Grant. Perhaps they narrowly missed a century of being Gruntfuttock…

THE TOAST OF AUSTRALIA: Dame Nellie Melba (above), an operatic soprano at the start of the 20th century, had, strangely, not one but four culinary treats named after her – Peach Melba, Sauce Melba, Melba Toast and Melba Garniture. Even odder, this wasn't her name – she was Helen Porter Mitchell, but used the stage name Melba in tribute to her home town, Melbourne in Australia. Pavlova was, however, really the name of the ballerina Anna (below) who inspired the dessert, created as a tribute, coincidentally, in Melbourne. She died in the same year as Melba, 1931.

22 Military mayhem: insane bungles and crackpot colonels

FATAL FLOORS: They were showing James II of Scotland the exciting new cannon at Floors Castle, near Kelso, in 1460, when it blew up, killing the King.

ADMIRAL'S BUNGLE: Sometimes a kid who's showing off in his new car gets it wrong and smashes up his pride and joy. That might have been the situation of the aptly-named Admiral Sir George Tryon, commanding the British Mediterranean fleet in 1893. He could have just had them anchor off Tripoli. But no, he had to take the ten enormous warships at high speed in two lines out from the coast in two columns of five, then turn towards each other, and steer shorewards. Then, after a sharp turn to travel parallel to the shore, the command 'anchor instantly' would have been flown from his signal halyard, and the moment it was hauled down ten blacksmiths would have hit ten wedges with ten sledgehammers, freeing ten huge anchors to drag ten heavy chains roaring out of their lockers to bring ten battleships or heavy cruisers to a sudden stop, all perfectly in line. Very impressive display of British naval power. Well, so he thought.

Except that the combined turning circle of two of these ships was 1,600 yards, so a safe distance would have been 2,400 yards. Tryon had left only 1,200 yards between the columns. None of the ten huge ship's captains dared query the flag-signalled command from this martinet, who liked to try daring and sudden manoeuvres to keep his men on their toes. Tryon was indeed trying it on and, like a boy racer doing a handbrake turn in front of the girls, was showing off. And some of the senior men thought he had a trick up his sleeve that would prevent disaster. He didn't; the two lead ships, *Victoria*, carrying Tryon and *Camperdown*, leading the other column, collided. *Victoria* sank, drowning 358 men, including, fortunately you may think, Tryon, who was blamed entirely for the disaster, disgracefully losing the latest warship named after the reigning monarch.

ANYONE ORDER ICE? An aircraft carrier built of ice was built in World War II, but on a landlocked Canadian lake. Mad British inventor Geoffrey Nathaniel Pyke suggested a ship made out of Pykrete, a mixture of ice and wood pulp, would be strong and unsinkable. The authorities needed somewhere with lots of water and wood, and chose central Canada for Project Habbakuk, as it would be the last place the Japanese would look for a secret aircraft carrier. It worked, oddly, but the fuel required to run the subsequent mile-and-a-half-long scaled up floating airbase – beating *Titanic's* iceberg at its own game, as it were – would have been colossal, so the cooling was switched off, it melted and the remains can be seen on the bottom of the lake.

THE ELITE French commando parachutists unit, the Commando de Renseignement et d'Action Profondeur, were puzzled by the lack of respect they received from some foreign armies. This may have been because they had acronym CRAP marked on their uniforms. It's been changed to Groupement de Commandos Parachutistes.

'TANKS' as a code-name for the military vehicles was devised to fool the Germans into thinking they were merely containers. The British Landship Committee was behind the project, and they were first used in 1916. After the Germans

captured one, they unfortunately got rather good at using landships by the next war. Or panzers, as they called them.

THE whole landships idea came because of the desperate need to break the murderous stalemate of trench warfare. An American magazine's idea included rather fancifully this:

THAT grenades are named after pomegranates, which they in some ways resembled inside and out, is obvious from the French word for the fruit: *grenade.* In World War I they were more dangerous to the throwers because the throwing hand would catch on the back of the narrow trench then drop it, (which was bananas). The British developed a grenade that also looked like a fruit, but not a pomegranate: The 'pineapple' (below).

THE RIGHT CALIBRE: With the millions of shots fired across the trenches in the First World War you'd think that someone would have got a bullet down the wrong end of a rifle. Well someone did. A British soldier was in his trench lining up to fire at a German sniper, and as he pulled the trigger felt an enormous blow that knocked him off the firing step. The two bullets had met halfway down the barrel (the German one being of a slightly smaller calibre), which bulged in a swelling at that point, the two projectiles fused together (the British Army has preserved the rifle). The soldier picked himself up but had no long-term damage; if the German's heart had beaten just at the wrong time and deflected the shot a tiny degree, he could have been dead. The German presumably went to his grave thinking he had killed that man.

ACCIDENT TYLER: On February 28, 1844, the U.S. Navy was showing off its new screw frigate, *USS Princeton*, hosting President 'Accident' John Tyler and members of the government (he'd got the nickname by taking over when the President suddenly died). They fired the ship's gun, which exploded, killing the Secretary of State, Thomas Gilmer, and the Secretary of Navy, Abel P. Upshur, and New York state senator David Gardiner. The latter's daughter Julia fainted and fell into the arms of the President. They later married. So 'Accident' Tyler gained two wonderful things by tragic accident.

FAREWELL SALUTE: At the beginning of the American Civil War, in April, 1861, Fort Sumter in Charleston harbour endured a bombardment of 36 hours during which more than 4,000 rounds were fired. No one was killed by all these shells, miraculously, and the fort surrendered. As the flags were hauled down at the surrender ceremony, a salute was fired and a cannon exploded, killing two men and injuring four.

PARATROOPS at the beginning of D-Day were dropped so low that their parachutes failed to open and they thudded into the ground and were killed. Others were dropped at the correct height onto flooded fields and drowned in their heavy kit. One American, John Steele, famously snagged his parachute on a church spire and survived only by feigning death while the battle raged beneath him. Yet others were mini-men dolls, with smaller parachutes, to fool Germans – you can't tell from the ground. They had firecrackers attached that went off when they landed to start apparent firefights.

ATOM BOMBS: Colonel Paul Tibbets who commanded the flight that dropped the first atom bomb on Hiroshima on August 6, 1945, incinerating many men, women and children and mortally wounding hundreds of thousands, had been born to drop things from planes, it seems. At 12, he had hitched his first ride in a plane with a stunt pilot dropping somewhat less dangerous free chocolate bars over Miami Beach. Tibbets had been given the job of chucking the sweets — each with its own little parachute — out of the cockpit of the tiny red-and-white biplane. He died in 2007, having seared his mother's name – Enola Gay – into the world's history because he named his bomber after her. There is no record of her ever objecting to being associated with the atomic mass slaughter. At the time, of course, it was regarded as a necessary thing (outside Japan) and saved millions of lives on both sides by ending the war.

FANCY A MUSHROOM CAKE (mushroom cloud, that is)? Given what atom bombs did to people – making their skin hang off like stripped wallpaper in Hiroshima, for example – you might not think a celebratory cake shaped like a mushroom cloud was in the best possible taste. But this is what Vice Admiral William Blandy enjoyed (pictured) after testing the U.S. H-bomb at Bikini atoll. His wife's hat wasn't that appealing either. In fact Blandy was angered at accusations of trivializing the issue, saying: 'I am not an atomic playboy.'

THE BRITISH showed the Japanese how to attack Pearl Harbor, although they didn't actually suggest this 1941 'day of infamy' that brought America into World War II. After the First World War the British pioneered the use of aircraft carriers and showed their then Japanese allies how to use them, selling them one. Then in 1940 the Royal Navy made a brilliant low level attack with torpedo planes on the Italian fleet in harbour at Taranto. The Japanese, then not at war, made full notes and sent a detailed report on how to sink a fleet at anchor in shallow waters. Bingo! Or rather, Banzai!

THE BRITS in fact sunk one of the American fleet that survived the Japanese attack at Pearl Harbor – but not very quickly. The light cruiser the *USS Phoenix* escaped the infamous 1941 attack unharmed. Decades later, she was sold to the Argentine Navy, and renamed the *General Belgrano*. After that country invaded the British-owned Falkland Islands in 1982, the ship was torpedoed by *HMS Conqueror*, thus finishing the job the Japanese aviators were trying to achieve 41 years before. The cruiser became the only ship in history – so far – to be sunk by a nuclear-powered submarine.

THE STUPID BRITS again did the Americans a bad turn at the end of World War II by giving their recent allies, the Soviets, a newly invented Rolls-Royce jet engine. Not long afterwards American propeller-driven aircraft in the Korean War were being shot down by the dozen by MiG jet fighters powered by very similar engines, which the Americans could not match for speed at the time. The Soviets had earlier confirmed the composition of the turbine blades by booking a tour of the Rolls-Royce factory at Derby, wearing foam-soled shoes and making sure they stood on the metal shavings in the engineering workshop, to copy the alloys used.

KAMIKAZE Japanese suicide pilots wore helmets, which seems odd as their planes were packed with explosives and were designed to explode on suicidal impact. The reason was that with helmets, they still felt and looked like pilots, and so their morale was kept up. Even odder, there was a need for a kamikaze pilot pension fund, as most of the pilots trained for this in the closing stages of World War II never made a real mission (there would be only one), and others were shot down or ran out of fuel. Whatever you think of the cause they were fighting for, they were staggeringly courageous, as film footage shows them flying through almost incredible walls of fire to reach their targets.

BAT BOMBS: The U.S. military developed a strange programme in World War II to drop bat bombs over Japan. Each bomb would contain thousands of live bats which would be released when it opened close to the ground. The bats would carry tiny incendiary bombs strapped to their legs and, come daybreak, would roost in nooks and crannies of the paper and wood houses of the Japanese cities. It was calculated this could be ten times more effective than just dropping incendiaries at random, and one of the experts predicted: 'Japan can be devastated, with very little loss of life'. (Bat life excepted, of course). The plan was coming along nicely when one of the canisters burst open at a U.S.

air base in New Mexico. The creatures fled to roost in dark places around the base – including fuel tanks and ammunition stores. Boom! This had other serious consequences – the setback delayed the plan long enough for the parallel atomic bomb programme to become the front-runner.

BALLOONATICS: An equally batty Japanese plan was to take advantage of the prevailing jetstream wind across the Pacific by launching balloons with small explosives attached and letting them drift across to America where they would descend and explode, causing mayhem. No need for long-range bomber aircraft, it would seem. And America would be crippled. The problem was that they were most likely to land in the ocean, or merely annoy an Alaskan bear, a Canadian moose or a Mexican mule rather than actually damage the American war machine. They were made of paper pasted together in halls by schoolchildren.

Oddly it worked – a bit. Some 10,000 were sent off and of these 285 were known to have exploded in the USA. Dreams of starting forest fires were thwarted by heavy rain. The only serious incident was when the family of an Oregon churchman picnicking in the woods found one of the objects. When a child tugged at the strings, all were killed. Tragic – particularly if you think of it as children killing children - but not a war-winning offensive.

A modern recreation of 'Dazzle' camouflage, on the River Thames

CUBISM AT WAR: In World War II Royal Navy captains were outraged to be ordered to paint their ships in garish cubist designs. However, given the submarine menace, this was a clever move. Seen through a periscope in poor weather, it was impossible to see the range of a ship or be certain where the bow was. Both were needed for setting torpedoes to run effectively. Thousands of lives were saved. This was an extension of World War I's equally garish 'Dazzle' camouflage (pictured above and below).

How to confuse a sub: Where is the bow of this ship?

23 Music: Instrument women weren't even allowed to listen to...

MUSICAL MONSTER: The world's first electric musical instrument was the Dynamophone, which weighed 200 tons, invented by American lawyer Thaddeus Cahill of Washington DC in 1897. It didn't perform publicly until 1906. It was electro-mechanical, with relays and switches moving parts, and required a large basement to be installed in plus a console at ground level. The instrument was also known as the Telharmonium (below). It took 30 railway cars to move it. The idea was (before amplification of music was possible), to make music centrally with a keyboard and distribute it over telephone wires, which the invention did in New York for a while. Restaurants, hotels and rich subscribers could for the first time have music without having to employ musicians (although it was always live from the Telharmonium, pictured, recording not being possible either).

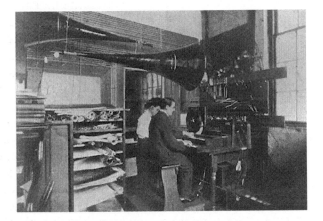

However ordinary telephone users were being pestered with a blast of Rossini – for example - in interference (as the cables were laid alongside), as was the U.S. Navy in its wireless transmissions. In the end the project fizzled out with the arrival of devices such as the Wurlitzer and Hammond organs (the latter owe technical details to their enormous predecessor) and then radio stations capable of transmitting real music wirelessly. At late as 1950 Thomas Cahill, the inventor's brother, was trying to find a museum for the third machine, but it went for scrap. However, the whole concept of piped music in lifts and shops is down to eccentric Thaddeus. Thanks a bunch, Thaddeus.

CONDUCTORS of orchestras sometimes look as if they might take someone's eye out with the jabbing, whirling baton, but one got so carried away that he killed himself. Jean-Baptiste Lully, also described as a dancer, composer and sodomite, was conducting for French King Louis XIV in 1687 when he hit his own foot so hard with his conducting staff that it was badly bruised, turned septic – yes, a musician decomposing. He died within two months.

THE UNITED STATES OF ARMONICA: The glass armonica, an instrument based on the principle that running your finger round a wet wine glass rim produces an ethereal sound, was invented by Benjamin Franklin, the same Franklin who helped invent independent America. He had heard the remarkable sound made by amateurs with ordinary glasses, so he had the stems of wine glasses drilled out (which must have been costly in breakages) and then mounted the bowls in ascending size on a horizontal spindle, which was rotated by the player using a treadle. The player then used wet fingers to produce the sounds.

The music is utterly extraordinary and was thought too emotionally dangerous for women to hear, and banned by some cities. It was feared that it would in some way hypnotise people or bring on madness. Ironically it possibly did cause madness, for it was found that the best glass had a very high lead content and the users would lick their fingers repeatedly. One player was found to have lead poisoning after a premature death. Later safer quartz crystal glasses were used. As for hypnotising people, the notorious Dr Franz Mesmer used it to mesmerise his patients. In the 21st century, however, the glass armonica, or glass harmonica (pictured), has been revived without women becoming hysterical or anyone going mad.

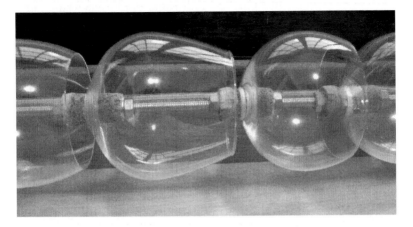

UKULELES were made in Portugal from at least as far back as 139BC, so why is their name Hawaiian? This arose when a Portuguese migrant brought the first instrument there in 1879 and the locals loved it, copied it, and renamed it the ukulele, which means 'jumping flea'.

WOULD YOU CREDIT IT? The Carpenters' most famous song, *We've Only Just Begun*, was, they admitted, inspired by a television commercial for a bank in California. The scene featured a newlywed couple who had only just begun their lives together, thanks to the bank. Richard Carpenter saw the TV commercial and sculpted it into the all-time romantic hit.

CHOPIN'S *Minute Waltz*, theme music for the BBC show *Just A Minute*, cannot be played in a minute, it lasts at least 90 seconds, possibly two minutes. But it's a publisher's nickname. Chopin had called it *The Little Dog Waltz*.

APT TUNES: Sometimes people choose horribly appropriate music deliberately – *Smoke Gets In Your Eyes* at a cremation, for instance. Other times it just happens. When London East End gangster Ronnie Kray shot dead George Cornell in 1966 through the eye at the Blind Beggar pub in London's Whitechapel, the juke box was playing *The Sun Ain't Gonna Shine Any More*. In the kerfuffle, the record stuck on the line 'shine any more'. The sun wasn't gonna shine any more for Cornell, said a cop.

BRILLIANT TRIBUTE BANDS (the names, if not the music): Surely Bassey, Not The Hoople, Fake That, Proxy Music, Kaiser Thiefs, The Stereophonies, Razorlike, Nearly Dan and the Rolling Clones.

THE song *You've Lost That Lovin' Feelin'* by the Righteous Brothers was played 8 million times on American radio stations during the 20th century, beating three other songs to the most-played in the century title: *Never My Love, Yesterday*, and *Stand By Me* all reached around 7 million. To play the winner non-stop that many times, on just one station, would have taken 45 years, needing 4,500 copies not to wear out that musical feelin'.

24 Sport: Anyone for Sphairistike?

LAWN TENNIS should be called called Sphairistike. It is a surprisingly recent British invention, having been patented by Major Walter Clopton Wingfield in 1874. He came up with the name from the Greek for ball, Sphaira, but the name didn't catch on as quickly as the game. It was intended for lawns with portable nets, so – confusingly – the game played on today's hard courts is still lawn tennis.

'REAL TENNIS' on the other hand involved a complicated indoor court and the 'real' meant Royal, as in Real Madrid football team. Appropriately, Henry VIII played it but in 1751 another prince who should have become king of England, Frederick, Prince of Wales, was killed by a tennis ball, the real tennis version being a lot heavier than the lawn tennis one.

THE new Victorian game of lawn tennis was a massive success with the British upper and middle classes, with ladies in long dresses playing in the 19th century and somewhat shorter outfits by the time poet John Betjeman was transfixed by player Joan Hunter Dunn. By the 1930s it was the quintessentially British middle-class suburban sport. Very polite, very middle class, very white.

CATGUT, formerly widely used for stringing tennis racquets and still for some, never contained real cat guts. The material, also used for bow strings in music, hanging weights in grandfather clocks and suturing wounds in surgery, was made from sheep guts, goat guts or pig guts (and occasionally, donkey guts). The word was a shortening of cattle-gut.

LOVE as a score in tennis stands for l'oeuf, meaning the egg in French, a humorous depiction of the figure 0. Deuce on the other hand means two – from the French deux – meaning two points required to win, not just one as normally at 40.

A ONE-ARMED MAN once played at the Wimbledon tennis tournament. In 1947, just two years after World War II ended, a former enemy of the Allies, Austrian player Hans Redl (pictured) was at Wimbledon - and applauded as a hero. He'd lost an arm at the horrendous Battle of Stalingrad, so the rules were changed so he could rest the ball on his racket and flip it in the air to serve. He reached the last 16 and was roundly applauded when he was knocked out. Not by the Russians this time.

THE ALL-ENGLAND CLUB in Wimbledon, home to world tennis, was founded as the All-England Croquet Club in 1868. It wasn't until 1875 that the words 'Lawn Tennis and' were inserted. It's still got croquet (illustrated above) in the name.

TENNIS ELBOW is hardly ever caused by tennis.

FOOTBALL fans in Britain are addicted to trivia. For instance, Hull City is the only club in the top 92 with no letters you can colour in, and in an even more staggeringly pointless waste of brain cells, Swindon Town in the only one with no letters shared with 'mackerel'.

THE FRONT CRAWL swimming style should be called the Trudgen. It was invented by Briton John Trudgen in 1873, although he got the idea from native Americans. It was disapproved of as un-British and undignified compared to less splashy breaststroke. No gentleman would try that hard, it was argued.

SWIMMING at all was first recommended in a 1538 book by German professor Nicholas Wynman, as a precaution against drowning, not as a sport. This could have been the thinking behind an event included in the first modern Olympics in 1896: 100 metres swimming *for serving sailors.*

THE ORIGINAL OLYMPIC GAMES were of course in Ancient Greece, but their modern revival in fact came with the Olympian Games held in Much Wenlock, Shropshire, England, from 1850, by a local doctor, William Penny Brookes. The international Olympics weren't started until 1896 by Frenchman Baron Pierre de Courbertin, who had visited the Much Wenlock games.

FLYING IN THE FACE OF IT: The discus (above) goes faster and further into the wind than with it.

ALL SPORTS except archery were technically illegal in England until 1960, whereas two hours a week of archery was compulsory. Henry V's 5,000 longbowmen wiped out a much larger French army at Agincourt in 1415, repeating the against-the-odds success of Edward III with archers at Crecy, also in France, in 1346. Edward made weekly archery

practice obligatory for men and boys in 1363 and banned all other sports. The law was formally repealed only in 1960.

THE MARATHON MARATHON: The length of the marathon race is popularly supposed to be the length run by the Ancient Greek messenger Pheidippides from the Battle of Marathon to bring the news of victory to Athens (and he dropped dead, remember?). It isn't: that was shorter. The Olympic distance was decided by an odd combination of pampered British royalty and a moody Italian volcano.

In 1908 the Italians were due to host the Olympics, but Vesuvius blew its top and they had their hands full. Any Italian marathon would have been a different distance, as that wasn't fixed until this 1908 race (or rather backdated to it - there were six different marathon distances in the first seven modern Olympics). London stepped in and the marathon was set to run from the Long Walk at Windsor Castle to the stadium at White City, exactly 25 miles (about 40km) by the route laid out. But then the Princess of Wales decided she wanted her children to watch the start so the start was moved round the Castle to the East Lawn, making it 26 miles. Then at the last moment it was decided that the athletes should run round the cinder track to the Royal Box to finish, just to please the royals, and the crowd, which added another 385 yards.

It's hard enough running the original 25 miles without an extra 1 mile 385yds, or 1 7/32 miles, added for some forgotten royals' convenience. In fact the metric conversions of this very peculiar distance have never been quite right. So in a close finish the winner might be different in metric or imperial – the variation is small but one day it could be crucial.

BALL'S BALL: The perfect shape for a golf ball was not round, aptly named Dunlop researcher Samuel Ball found in a scientific study, but covered with exactly 332 dimples 0.13in deep, which made it fly much further and straighter. His design became the standard.

GOLF CADDY: The golf term caddy comes from using a trainee officer or cadet, pronounced in French *cadday*, to carry your clubs. And golf links, that is make-do beach courses, were invented when a Scottish king banned proper golf courses to encourage practice at archery.

BOXING RINGS: Are always in fact square, because of the need to put ropes up. Once it would have been a circle of spectators, hence ring.

TEAM SELECTION: The number of possible permutations for the batting order of one team of 11 cricketers is 39,916,800. This is easy compared with selecting the first four moves in chess, which has 318,979,564,000 permutations.

CHECKMATE in chess comes from the Persian *Shah Mat*, which means 'the king is dead'.

A TOUGH TUG O' WAR would be required to pull two people's arms off, you'd think. But this was the outcome of a mass tug o' war in Taipei, Taiwan on October 25, 1997. Some 1,600 people joined in the national holiday event, using a 5cm diameter nylon rope with a certified breaking strain of 26 tons. The estimated effort was 80 tons, and the result was that the rope snapped with such force that it took two men's arms off. Tug o' war (below) was an Olympic event from 1900-1920.

25 Wildlife & nature: Beasts beyond belief

GILBERT WHITE, the 18th century English 'father of natural history' whose book *The Natural History of Selborne* still draws people to that Hampshire village, thought that swallows disappeared in winter because they dived to the bottom of ponds and hid in the mud.

DOLPHINS go to sleep with one half of their brain at a time, and one eye closed. Sounds like a student trying to drive home from the pub …

BUTTERFLIES taste with their feet.

MALE BRIMSTONE butterflies were once the only *'butter flie'*, being yellow - the name spread to other species. Brimstone is an old name for sulphur, which the butterflies (below) match in colour even more closely than butter.

FOR TORTOISES to live their 150-plus years they must never once fall on their backs.

EELS can't live underwater without coming up for air but can swim effectively backwards.

IF YOU drop alcohol on a scorpion (below) it goes mad and stings itself to death.

IF YOU intoxicate an ant, it always falls on its left side.

AN albatross can sleep while it flies. It dozes off while cruising at 25 mph. This is how they survive thousands of miles from land. Guinea pigs don't come from Guinea and aren't pigs.

AN ADDER for a snake is wrong. It should be a nadder. (See orange, Page 37)

RHYME AND REASON: *A woman, a whippet, a walnut tree. The more you beat them, the better they be.* This deeply unpleasant country rhyme is true in one respect, with an application in the moneyed gin and Jag belt. Intrigued? It is obviously nonsense about women; doubtful about whippets; and also stupid about the walnuts you eat. No measurable gain in the number of nuts has been found from beating a walnut tree. But walnut as a wood is attractive, strong and light. It is used for the stocks of guns and dashboards of posh cars – the above mentioned Jaguars, for example. For this purpose, it is more decorative if it has lots of swirls in the grain. These are caused by injuries when growing. Such as by being beaten with chains or sticks.

ALL JUMBO jets or jumbo anything, meaning big, owe their name to Jumbo the African elephant who was exhibited in France in 1861, then at London Zoo where he gave children rides, and then joined the Barnum & Bailey Circus in North America. He was killed by a locomotive in a railway yard at St Thomas, Ontario, Canada in 1885 – circuses in those days travelled by their own trains. That town has a life-size statue.

WHALE WAY ACCIDENT: A 60-ton, 56ft long sperm whale exploded in a shopping street in Taiwan in 2004. Gas from internal decay caused the explosion. The whale, which had beached itself, was being taken on a flatbed truck to a university for examination. No one was hurt, but blood, flesh and rotting entrails showered cars and shops, and the stench was appalling.

SEALS swallow large pebbles and keep them in their stomachs throughout their lives. They use them to break down shellfish and any other tough pieces in their diet.

BUGGING YOU: For every person on the planet there is 300 times their body weight in insects, or by another estimate 200 million insects. And if you've been beside a Scottish loch in late summer, you begin to believe it.

BRIGHTLY COLOURED birds don't exist. Well, that's an over simplification, but the most such birds aren't coloured at all. There is a strange microscopic grid over their feathers which allows only certain wavelengths through, giving the impression of a brilliant colour. That's why the colours on a peacock or a male mallard appear brilliant, but work only at certain angles of viewing. Why, no one knows.

LONG DROP: A mother giraffe gives birth standing up, so the baby falls about 6ft. Tough start.

QUICK SCAN: Like barcodes, all zebra are differently patterned. A member of the Rothschild family trained four zebra to pull his carriage around the English countryside and London (below). A cross between a male zebra and another equine is a zedonk, the other way round is a donkra.

MOUSE sperm are longer than elephant sperm. Lions can mate 50 times a day.

NECKING: Giraffes have the same number of vertebrae as cats, humans and dolphins.

ONE in 50,000 penguins is hatched with brown not black plumage. These are called Isabelline penguins. Sounds a lovely name? Er, no. It is a reference to the story that the Archduchess Isabella of Austria vowed not to change her undergarments until her husband united the northern and southern Low Countries by taking the city of Ostend – which took three years.

TALKING about penguins and unmentionable stains, Adelie penguins' habitats can be tracked from space by looking for pink areas of ice. That's because they eat krill, a shrimp.

ALL polar bears are left handed. Land and sea creatures near the poles are bigger than elsewhere.

POLAR BEARS can swim about 60 miles (which they may need to increasingly). Elephants can also swim (below) miles out to sea, although even with global warming the chances of the two meeting are low.

TALK of polar bears becoming extinct due to global warming is a bit overdone, says one scientist: 'Polar bears will not become extinct, they will just go back to what they were, which is brown bears.' This is the reverse of what happens when stoats become ermine in the winter (when their coats become pure white, unfortunately for them, because then British peers, kings, Catholic monarchs and cardinals all want to make robes out of them). It's a stoat funeral for them…

WHEN a polar bear breeds with a grizzly, the result is a Pizzly.

SHEEP and other herbivores have horizontal pupils so they can keep an eye on predators coming from the sides; cats have vertical pupils because they need to focus on prey; humans have round pupils because our eyes are far enough off the ground for it not to matter but also to make us all-round successful hunters and tool users.

26 Quotations: Why we get them so wrong

QUOTES WE ALL *'KNOW'* FULL WELL ... BUT ARE COMPLEET ERRERS!

'Play it again, Sam' Film *Casablanca* (above). In fact: 'Play it, Sam. Play As Time Goes By'.

'It's life, Jim, but not as we know it.' *Star Trek.* **In fact: 'It's life, Captain, but not life as we know it'.**

'Beam me up, Scotty.' *Star Trek.* In fact: 'Beam us up, Mr Scott.'

'Let them eat cake.' Marie Antoinette, commonly held as proof that the French Queen understood little when told the poor 'have no bread'. It was said at least 19 years before she was born. And the quotation is 'Qu'ils mangent de brioche' which was an alternative type of bread, not cake.

'Elementary, my dear Watson.' *Sherlock Holmes.* From 1929 film. Never said it.

'You dirty rat.' *James Cagney.* **Never said.**

'Rivers of blood.' *Enoch Powell* . In fact: 'Like the Roman, I seem to see "the River Tiber foaming with much blood".'

'Alas poor Yorick, I knew him well.' *Shakespeare, Hamlet.* **In fact: 'Alas, poor Yorick! I knew him Horatio – a fellow of infinite jest, of most excellent fancy.'**

'Discretion is the better part of valour.' *Shakespeare Henry IV, pt 1* In fact: 'The better part of valour is discretion.'

'Do you feel lucky, punk?' *Clint Eastwood, Dirty Harry.* **In fact: 'You have to ask yourself one question, punk. Do you feel lucky?'**

'Mirror, mirror on the wall, who is the fairest of them all?' *Snow White (1937).* In fact: 'Magic Mirror on the Wall, who is the Fairest one of all?'

'And not a lot of people know that.' *Michael Caine.* **In fact: 'Not many people know this.'**

QUOTES WE *TOTALLY* MISUNDERSTAND

Brevity is the soul of wit. *Taken to mean:* Tell jokes quickly. *In fact means:* A serious message is best said quickly (Polonius, bringing bad news). It means wit as in end of one's wits, or dimwit. *Not* humour.

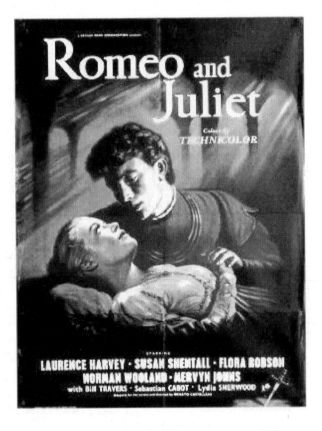

Wherefore art thou Romeo? *Taken to mean:* Where are you Romeo? *In fact means:* Why do you have to be who you are, Romeo – as in Julius Caesar 'Wherefore rejoice?' Or the modern phrase 'the whys and the wherefores'.

The exception which proves the rule. (not Shakespeare but in general) *Taken to mean:* Let's highlight an exception. *In fact* *means:* Legally if there's an exception, it implies a rule. A sign warning 'No trucks over 25 tons across this bridge' implies it is a right of way for lighter vehicles. The origin is a Latin maxim, *exceptio probat regulam in casibus non exceptis* (the exception confirms the rule in cases not excepted).

Salad days. *Taken to mean:* Best days. *In fact means:* Foolish or green inexperience. Cleopatra says: 'My salad days, When I was green in judgement; cold in blood'.

Head over heels. *Taken to mean:* Upside down. *In fact means:* Normal way up. But originally people said heels over head, then someone made an error and it stuck because it's easier to say.

Weakest go to the wall. *Taken to mean:* Sadly the weak can't last. *In fact means:* From medieval churches where services were compulsory and lasted for three or more hours, and there were no pews, it was said 'Let the weakest go the wall' so they could lean on something. So it means help the weak, opposite to most people's understanding.

East is East and West is West, and never the twain shall meet. *Taken to mean:* That the two sets of people will never understand each other. *In fact means:* The poem is a 'Straw Man' argument - setting up a point of view and then knocking it down as nonsense. Kipling (below) says it doesn't make any difference when it matters. The first line here is almost sarcastic.

'Oh, East is East and West is West, and never the twain shall meet,
Till Earth and Sky stand presently at God's great judgment Seat;
But there is neither East nor West, Border, nor Breed, nor Birth,
When two strong men stand face to face, though they come from the
ends of the earth!'

27 Words: There's a magic spell in them

WORDS THAT DON'T EXIST: People commonly say there isn't a word for the plastic cover on the end of a shoelace. There is. It's an aglet.

GENDER BLENDER AGENDA: In recent years words such as *actor* have tended to be increasingly used for both sexes, making *actress* less common. This has suited some people's gender blender agenda. Certainly *aviatrix* seems old-fashioned now for female aviator, although *dominatrix* is still needed because it tells you rather more about the situation than mere dominator. This leads on to:

WHY WOMEN CAN'T BE SENATORS: In fact the process of merging gender-specific words is old. The female of brethren was sistren. Females could not go senile, but went anile, suffering from anileness/anility. That's because *senex* is Latin for old man. Therefore senators, who attend a senate (*senatus* in Latin) are old men, literally. Not women or young people. About 50 countries have senates, and in a nod to the Latin, they are usually the senior house, although not exclusively male. So Hillary Clinton should have been an *anilatrix*, not a senator.

ALUMINUM: This entry is purely to make Americans feels better at what could be perceived as British smugness about the language. Aluminum is correct. Some poncy British twerp thought it would sound better matching the other metals, such as chromium, etc, and stuck the 'I' in which forces the Brits to stress the third syllable in aluminium not the second, which was correct. Too bad. The British spelling has become accepted outside America. Still wrong.

MAVERICK comes from a reaction against branding. Not company names but real branding of animals, as in fire brand. After the American Civil War, Texas rancher Samuel Maverick noticed that all his neighbours carefully branded their cattle. He decided his animals would therefore stand out if they were not branded. In breaking with convention, Maverick was the first maverick. Neologisms run in this family: his grandson Maury Maverick invented the word 'gobbledygook', imitating the noise of turkeys, to complain about the language of bureaucrats in 1944.

HAZARD AHEAD could be a good thing. A hazard should really be an accident, a chance, good or bad. It comes from the Arabic *Al zahr,* the dice (or die correctly in the singular, as in the die is cast), and *hazard* was used only for a dice game in Europe for many centuries.

GALLANT, on the other hand, does not, or did not, mean a good thing. It meant as a noun a showy ladies' man, an over-dressed paramour, someone who was all front and no honour. So today an award 'for gallantry' should pedantically meant 'for being a puffed up, insincere flirt'. By extension it had come to be applied to a fine-looking thing such as a ship, and then back to people as brave. Meanwhile the ladies' man meaning was diluted down to merely courteous.

NOON means the ninth hour, not the twelfth. It is derived from the Latin *nona hora,* the ninth hour of the day. The Roman day started at 6am, at sunrise. As they had no zero, that would make their noon at 2pm. The Roman hours were vital in medieval monasteries, where prayers were said according to them.

MONTHS are wrong too. Clearly, September, October. November and December means seventh, eighth, ninth and tenth month, whereas they are actually two months on from that. The culprits were the preceding two months, named after pushy Roman emperors, Julius Caesar and Augustus.

FRENCH FART: The name for the new *GEC-Plessey Telecommunications* giant created in France in 1988 was GPT. These initials were erected in huge letters over

factories etc. It was a disaster as French giggled helplessly every time they said it. It sounded like 'J'ai pété' or 'I've farted'.

PUT A SOCK IN IT meaning 'please quieten down' originates from wind-up gramophones which, being entirely mechanical, had no volume control. The only way to mute the sound was to stuff a sock in the large horn that was connected to the needle.

ALCATRAZ: Albatross the bird is a mispronunciation of Alcatraz, an old Portuguese word for big bird. So Birdman of Alcatraz means Birdman of Big Bird.

SERENDIPITY: The Persian for Sri Lanka was Serendip, and a fairytale talked of three princes discovering wonderful things by chance - the chance element must figure in the modern meaning of serendipity, a happy discovery. It was taken up as a word in English by gothic novelist Horace Walpole, who is recorded using it in 1754. Like all new words, it would stay if there was a regular need for it, and disappear if there wasn't. There was.

SERENDIPITY, continued: The word said by experts to be the hardest English word to translate, so nearly every language has imported it. Except, *of course*, the French, who officially at any rate are supposed to use *heureux hasard*.

ZEMBLANITY: Is the opposite of serendipity, unhappy discoveries made while trying to find something else. It was coined by William Boyd and relates to the island of Novaya Zemlya in the Arctic where the explorer Willem Barents was stuck. It is hostile, useless and barren, quite unlike Sri Lanka. There probably isn't a regular need for this word, so it probably won't stick.

FRENCH BEAK: The avocet is a black and white bird (above) and the word comes from the French for lawyer. So 'up before the beak' is appropriate. The fact that the bill is longer and higher than reasonable may be just a coincidence. The black and white New Zealand bird known as a *tui* to Maori was similarly called the parson bird by British settlers.

WORDY BIRDY: More wondrous wordy connections come with another black and white bird, the magpie. There is a disease found in medical dictionaries called Pica, which is defined as 'a perverted craving for substances unfit to be used as food' – a child who eats dirt all the time, or a pregnant woman who eats coal or something similar. The Latin for magpie, a bird which would indeed glean unsuitable things and steal stuff, is *pica*, same as the disease. That word was there first, so the human disease means being magpie like. Bizarrely sometimes the children with pica have real diet problems like an iron deficiency and this is their instinctive way of desperately trying to fix it.

PIEBALD also means magpie like, and nothing to do with being bald. It describes someone or some animal having a surprising probably white streak of hair at the forehead, or blotches of colour in general. Pie means like a magpie and bald is of Welsh origin, meaning a white streak on the forehead. The Welsh for oystercatcher means 'sea pie'.

SHAMBLES: Originally meant, and in places like York still does mean, a place for butchering animals, full of gore and mess. By extension anything chaotic is thought of as shambolic.

HOMOSEXUAL AND LESBIAN: The word homosexual has nothing to do with the Latin *homo*, meaning man, as in *homo sapiens*. It is from the Greek *homo* meaning the same, as in homogenous. So a lesbian is homosexual, and the phrase 'homosexual and lesbian' is tautology. Queen Victoria famously refused to sign a law against lesbianism because she didn't believe such an activity was possible. In 1921 Lord Birkenhead helped throw out a Bill to criminalise lesbianism, which probably saved a lot of pointless bother. Birkenhead said that 999 women out of 1,000 had 'never even heard a whisper of these practices'. They have now, chum.

TYPEWRITER: Is the longest word that can be made using the letters only on one row of a standard keyboard, and stewardesses is the longest word typed with only the left hand.

PANGRAM: A sentence that contains every letter in the alphabet, and they are useful for typing exercises, testing keyboards or equipment such as Telex printers, or trying out new fonts (people can get quite faddy about fonts, leading to comments such as 'Isn't that g in Souvenir bold *magnificent*? But the upper case I is just ridiculous!')

THE best known example of a pangram (see last item) is
The quick brown fox jumps over the lazy dog

But a shorter one is

Waltz, bad nymph, for quick jigs vex.

It is almost impossible to have one sentence that makes much sense without some repetition of characters. But a perfect pangram, that is an anagram of the alphabet, is:

Mr. Jock, TV quiz PhD, bags few lynx.

OTHER languages have their own pangrams (see last item). For example, French:

Portez ce vieux whisky au juge blond qui fume.

Which means 'take this old whisky to the blond judge who smokes'. It's those amiable avocets again (see above).

A Dutch version:

De export blijft qua omvang typisch zwak

(the amount of export remains typically weak).

Oddly, typographers still use a Latin one in the 21st century.

Lorem ipsum dolor sit amet, consectetur adipiscing elit,

diam nonnumy eiusmod tempor incidunt ut labore et dolo...

Odd in that Latin had only 23 letters, so it doesn't do the full job, and it is a late medieval typesetting bit of dog Latin that doesn't even make sense, being a mangled part of a quotation from Cicero that should read

Neque porro quisquam est qui dolorem ipsum

quia dolor sit amet, consectetur, adipisci velit...

Meaning

There is no one who loves pain itself, who seeks after it, and wants to have it, simply because it is pain...

Which pretty well sums up the position of typesetters expected to set this in perhaps eight different type sizes and a dozen different fonts (which in moveable metal type days, wasn't as quick as a brown fox jumping over a lazy dog).

The reasons why it is still used are perhaps: craftsman have always liked to use a closed language to show how learned they are and exclude others, as with doctors, priests and lawyers using Latin; and also that the type if filling in a headline or caption space is obviously nonsense whereas some smart aleck joke about the typesetter's ugly backside, for example, could accidentally end up being published. You still see dummy pages filled with that cod Latin text today in magazines and newspapers just as in 15th century typesetters.

P&Qs: That last activity led to the expression 'minding your Ps and Qs'. In lower case, and backwards in metal type, ps and qs are very easy to mix up but expensive to rectify after printing reveals the error. By the way, if you have never seen old-fashioned type, this picture shows: db (top) and qp.

UNANSWERABLE: Why is abbreviation such a long word? Why does onomatopoeia not sound like anything? Why is there no other word for Thesaurus? Why does saying out loud the abbreviation 'www' take three times as long as saying 'world wide web' that it's supposed to be flaming well short for?

IRRITABLE VOWELS: What's odd about the following sentence, apart from being nearly nonsense? 'Facetious, abstemious Sebastian considered the rhythm hymn Sequoia uncomplimentary, unoriental.' The first two words contain all the English vowels in the correct order, the last two all of them in reverse order and the shortest well-known word containing all of the vowels precedes those two. The two words before that have no full vowels (y being a half-vowel). There is a shorter, little used word containing all the vowels: Eunoia means a well mind, proper mental functioning and appears in medical dictionaries. It does exist: Eu- meaning good as in Eulogy, -oia state of mind, as in paranoia.

UNCOPYRIGHTABLE: The only 15-letter English word that does not repeat any letters is probably uncopyrightable, because it *is* uncopyrightable. Subbookkeeper is the only English word with four pairs of double letters in a row.

STEALING SOMEONE'S THUNDER: Started with English playwright John Dennis (1657-1734) complaining that the performance of *Macbeth* which followed his own play had much better thunder effects.

A FACTOID ABOUT FACTOIDS: Originally and logically things that were *like* facts but not facts (as humanoids are *like* humans but not humans), ie untrue but believed by many people (for example, that Teflon was created by the space programme) but in recent years it has been applied by people including BBC Radio 2 to facts that are facts, but are interesting but useless. Like those in this book. Fact: they are wrong.

FASCINATING ACRONYMS: *Mafia* is an acronym – morte alla francia, italia adela: Death to the French is Italy's cry. *Taser* is a weird acronym coming from a 1911 book *Tom Swift and His Electric Rifle* by Victor Appleton. 'Tom A Swift and his Electric Rifle' was used to give us Taser, name of the gun that fires two barbs on wires charged with thousands of volts. It's even become a verb – 'police tasered the suspect' and Americans cops say 'Stop or I will tase you.' No doubt it succeeded as a word because it sounds like a better known acronym *Laser* (**Light Amplification by Stimulated Emission of Radiation**). But taser is, in truth, a *backronymn* - one where you start with the name and then find words to fit.

EQUALLY there were two submarine detection systems devised during the Second World War on either side of the Atlantic, *Asdic* in Britain (supposedly from Allied Submarine Detection Investigation Committee) and *Sonar* (SOund NAvigation and Ranging) in America. *Sonar* stuck, probably because it sounds like *Radar* (RAdio Detection And Ranging). The latter has been more recently adapted for the ability to sense whether or not someone is homosexual: *gaydar*.

MORE ACRONYMS: Pakistan is an acronym for Punjab, Afghania, Kashmir and Sind, with the back end from Beluchistan (although this was possibly adapted from a 1930s Cambridge Muslim students' proposal for a 'pure land' – *Pak Stan*). The Soho area of New York stands for South of Houston, whereas Soho in London was the hunting cry in these woods, then well west of the city. The Australian airline Qantas stood for Queensland And Northern Territories Air Service. Zip in Zip Code sounds speedy, luckily, but in fact stood for Zoning Improvement Plan.

WARTIME ACRONYMS: Although acronyms weren't used much by civilians until the late 20th century, they were much loved by the military before that. And soldiers took to them for romantic purposes. Letters would be finished with BURMA - Be Upstairs Ready My Angel. MALAYA - My Ardent Lips Await Your Arrival. EGYPT - Eager to Grab Your Pretty Tits NORWICH - (k)Nickers Off Ready When I Come Home HOLLAND - Hope Our Love Lasts And Never Dies ITALY - I'm Thinking About Loving You or I Trust And Love You. These were eagerly decoded at home with the help of other Army wives and/or sweethearts. The geographical theme caused consternation to censors.

SWALK - Sealed With A Loving Kiss – was another romantic wartime acronym put on the back of envelopes, and later made a film title, but one British soldier challenged by the censor to explain it said it stood for Soldiers Will Always Love The King. Problem solved. BOLTOP meant Better On Lips Than On Paper. An American WWII acronym that has entered the language is SNAFU, meaning something had gone wrong, standing for Situation Normal: All Fouled Up. Or a ruder word than 'Fouled'.

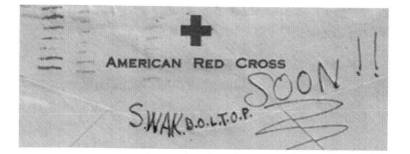

TRIVIUM ABOUT TRIVIA: The origins of this word are equally split two ways, not three ways (which is what it means in Latin). It either means three roads, and by extension street corner gossip, vulgar and common, but interesting, as you would find at a stall at such a corner. Or the three ways to less important knowledge in ancient universities, in which case it means knowledge that is of interest to the learned and inquisitive, but not essential to high-level learning. That sounds more like the modern trivia. The three subjects that were trivial lower level were grammar, rhetoric and logic. And if those were trivial, clearly celebrity culture hadn't been invented yet.

QUADRIVIUM: The four ways of upper knowledge in ancient universities were arithmetic, astronomy, geometry and music. If the trivium subjects gave us the adjective trivial, could not the quadrivium subjects and anyone being serious be *quadrivial*?

WIFE-BEATER is the unpleasant American slang for the sleeveless undervest as made famous by Marlon Brando in the movie *A Streetcar Named Desire* - his abused wife was Stella. In Britain 'wife-beater' is also unfortunate slang for a very good but strong lager beer, also oddly called Stella. Both names were doubtless coined with ironic humour in a younger rebellious generation way, not associating those products with any real intent.

GOING ROUND THE BEND: Is a British expression for becoming insane. Few people recall its origin – that the huge 19th century lunatic asylums were built with a curve in their approach drives so the passing public were spared the sight of lunatics, as they were then termed. So if you went round the bend, you had indeed gone mad.

'METEORIC RISE' describing a career is nonsense. They fall. If they become a big cheese, it's *chiz*, Hindi for 'thing', not cheese.

CLOUD CUCKOO LAND: How old is this expression, meaning an unrealistically ideal state? A 1970s politician, perhaps? *Peter Pan,* a century ago? No, it's 2,400 years old and comes in a Greek play by Aristophanes, in which Mr Trusting and Mr Hopeful, tired of Earth and Olympus, decide to build a perfect city, called Cloud Cuckoo Land.

WHY WE GO HAYWIRE: Hay bales used to be round and tied with a thin wire, also used for fence repairs. This stuff, once undone from its coil, sprang out crazily and became so entangled as to be useless unless expertly handled.

TALKING OUT OF URANUS: Astrology means the study of the stars, and columnists indeed say they discuss what 'the stars tell you'. They in fact discuss which *planets* are apparently moving about, relative to the fixed stars. They discuss very little, for some reason, the two things that clearly *do* influence things on Earth – the Sun and the Moon which twice daily move billions of tons of water around in the tides on this planet. The last thing they discuss is stars.

CLEAVE is said to be the only verb in English that has two meanings that are contranyms or antonyms, that is opposites: adhere and separate: The animal cleaved to its mother, but it had a cloven hoof.

SEVERAL other words can in a way be their opposites. Consider: I clipped it from the newspaper and then clipped it to the noticeboard. Children should be screened from this film screening. John is desk-bound today, but Mary is bound for the big city. When Mary has left, John is left.

NO WORDS rhyme with orange, famously, nor purple or silver. But if proper nouns are allowed, one *does* with the former: A hill in South Wales called the Blorenge.

LEWD comes from lay, meaning not a priest.

STUDENTS WHO ARE PROUDLY HALF STUPID: Sophomores, which are second year students particularly in

America, are telling the world they are still half stupid. A writer in the late 17th century humorously described those who were between a *fresher* and a *soph* or *Sophister* (senior student, more sophisticated, not yet taking finals) as *sophomores*. This was half derived from the Greek *moros*, stupid, foolish, as in moron, and the term stuck for those between wisdom and stupidity.

WOODEN SPOON: This now common phrase for a figurative award to he or she who comes last in anything – used in sports reports the world over – recalls the real wooden spoon which was lowered from the gallery at the Senate House in Cambridge as the very last maths degree was awarded. It used to be in fact a malting shovel, and it was traditionally inscribed with the name, date and college arms of the recipient (rather as oars are emblazoned for rowers). The Wooden Spoon and its holder were carried round the town as an honour for being dunce of the degree. At times the Wooden Spoon was a massive ornamental thing 5ft long, and was dangled twisting over the recipient like the Sword of Damocles. Some are preserved in colleges, such as St John's, which has the last, awarded in 1909 and inscribed in Greek. See Wrangler (next) for the opposite.

WRANGLER: Nothing to do with the denim jeans, but the term for those who achieve first class honours in maths at Cambridge. The second class honours are senior and junior *optimes*. The highest mark of all goes to the Senior Wrangler, an honour indeed. I say nothing to do with jeans, but there is a link, just about. *Wrangle,* a German-derived word, has two meanings in English. To wrestle with and dispute in the hope of overcoming (presumably the origin of wranglers at Cambridge and an intransitive verb, you wrangle with somebody, you don't wrangle somebody) and an American transitive verb, to wrangle cattle (again wrestling to overcome them, hence a cowboy term, a cattle *wrangler*). That must be where the jeans and the Jeep Wrangler car come from.

DERRICK for a type of crane and tawdry, as in a cheap necklace, both relate to real people – a 17th-century chap called Derrick who had such a crane (which he used to hang people) and St Audrey, a queen of Northumbria who had such a necklace.

A SILHOUETTE and to boycott are also eponyms, words derived from a name. Étienne de Silhouette was a Frenchman known for frugality, and thus his name was taken in 1759 for a cheap new form of portrait. In the 1800s Irish tenant farmers vowed to have absolutely no dealings of any sort with a land agent, Charles C. Boycott, sent to evict them. They were the first to boycott someone.

ARGHH! Panophobia is the fear of everything.

HIPPOPOTOMONSTROSESQUIPEDALIOPHOBIA: Is, somewhat insensitively you may feel, the word for an irrational fear of people using long words. Or – look away now, sufferers! - being sesquipedalianally circumlocutory. That is, using long words long-windedly. Which is a good place to stop!

ABOUT THE AUTHOR

Benedict le Vay is a London-born journalist, author and 'rather bad yachtsman and potter' who has worked as a newspaper sub-editor in major newspapers in Britain, Hong Kong and New Zealand. A father of two, his books have included the best-selling *Eccentric Britain, Eccentric London, Eccentric Oxford* and *Eccentric Cambridge* guides, and also *Britain From The Rails: A Window-Gazer's Guide*, all published by Bradt, plus *Weeping Waters: When Train Meets Volcano*. Asked if he himself is eccentric, he says: 'Not at all, I'm afraid. The best I can do is being Honorary Secretary of the Friends of the A272, and asking for my ashes to be blasted from the chimney of my favourite steam loco at my funeral. But then hasn't everyone?'

Picture: WENDY FULLER

BEST-SELLERS BY THE SAME AUTHOR

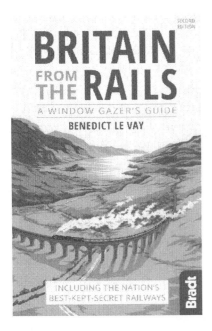

Real reader reviews: Now, finally, the network has a book to be proud of - I love how Benedict le Vay gives a detailed explanation on a huge variety of railway lines throughout the country, be it main line, commuter or country branch lines, but always with a good smattering of humour in there to make you want to read on.

A masterpiece!

My husband loves this book. You could hear him laughing and he would share tidbits with me.

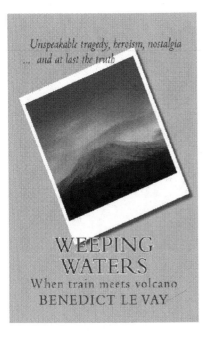

Published on Amazon. Press reviews:

Sixty years on, le Vay's masterly reconstruction is a fine memorial.- *Jane Mays, Daily Mail, London*

He has researched the story well and tells it with great passion, making the full facts public for the first time. - *The Railway Magazine, UK.*

International must-read. - *Dominion-Post, Wellington, New Zealand*